THE SECRET LIFE
OF MARY JAMES,
WELSHWOMAN

In memory of William Andrew James
'Andy'

29 August 1951—11 March 2023

Crumps Barn Studio
Syde, Cheltenham GL53 9PN
www.crumpsbarnstudio.co.uk

Cover design and maps by Lorna Gray

All photographs © the author unless otherwise specified

Typeset in Adobe Garamond Pro

All our books are printed on responsibly sourced paper from managed woodlands.
Printed in the UK by CMP, Poole.

ISBN 978-1-915067-47-0

THE SECRET LIFE OF MARY JAMES, WELSHWOMAN

DIARIES 1916—1920

edited by

SIAN JENNINGS

Crumps Barn Studio

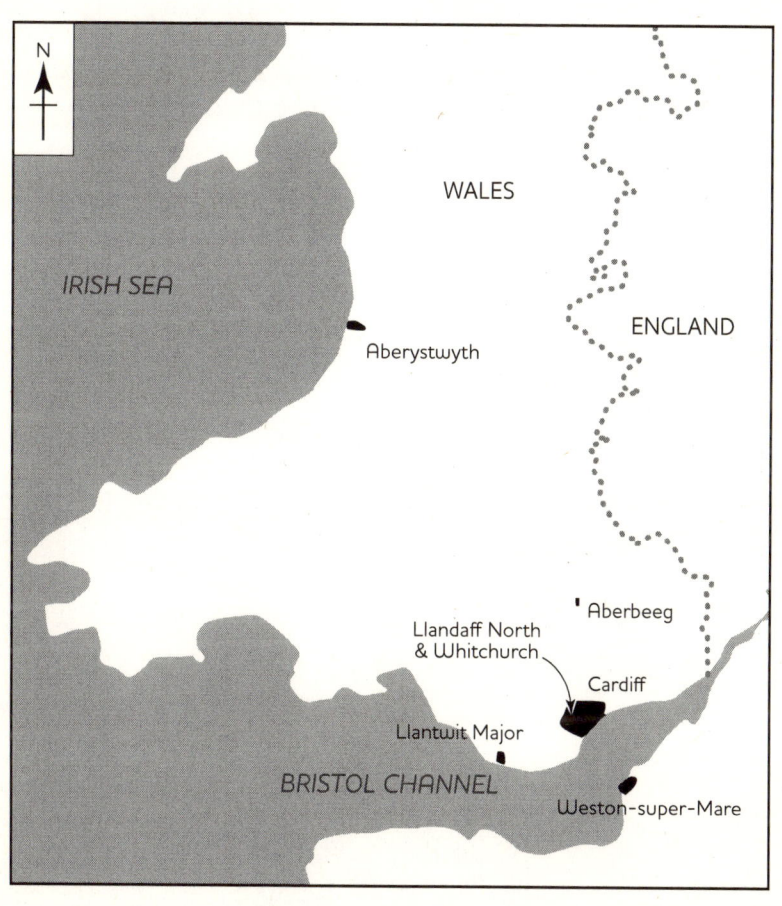

Map of the area (not to scale)

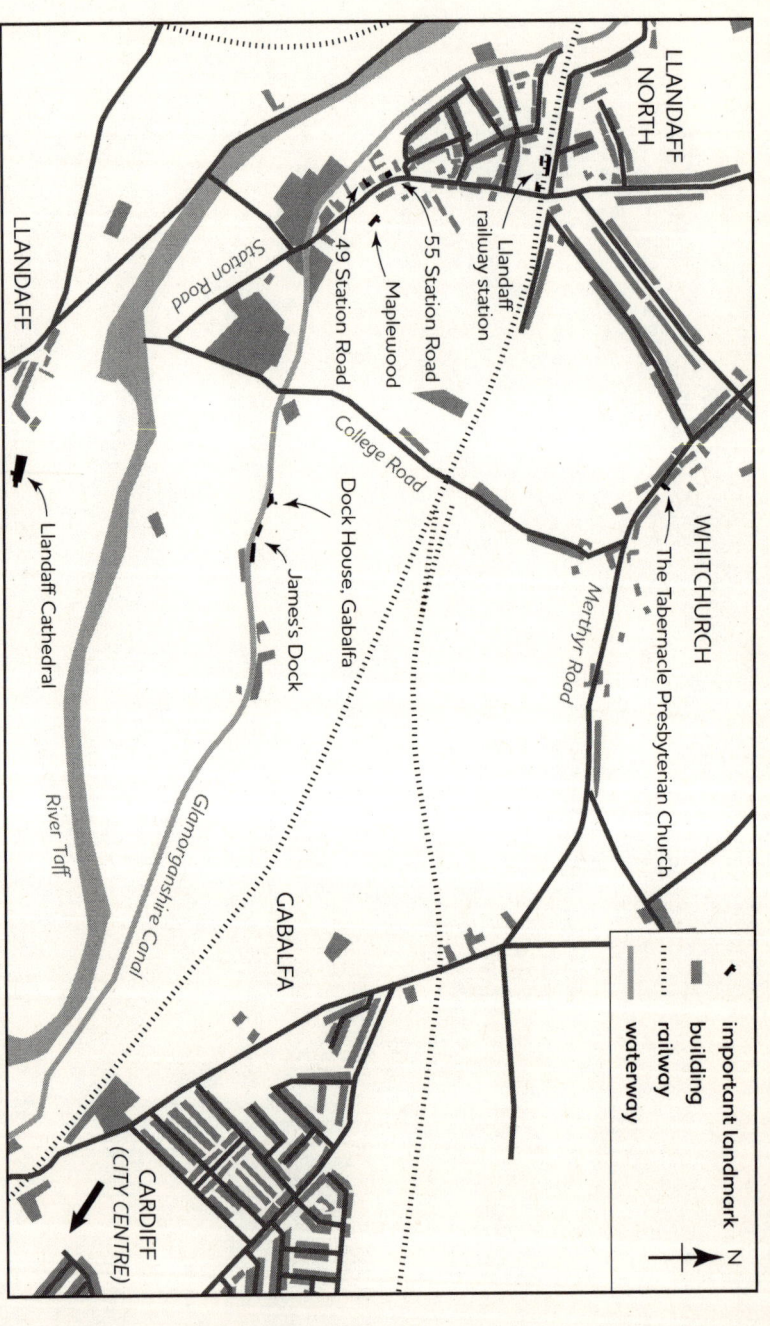

Map of the principal locations (not to scale)

LLANDAFF NORTH

LLANDAFF

Station Road

Llandaff railway station

55 Station Road

Maplewood

49 Station Road

College Road

Merthyr Road

WHITCHURCH

The Tabernacle Presbyterian Church

Dock House, Gabalfa

James's Dock

Llandaff Cathedral

River Taff

Glamorganshire Canal

GABALFA

CARDIFF (CITY CENTRE)

important landmark
building
railway
waterway

N

INTRODUCTION

MARY JAMES was born on 8 July 1902 at 55 Station Road, Llandaff North, Cardiff. She was the first child of William Gwalchmai James, a building contractor, and his wife Hannah Candina, formerly Andrews. Mary's siblings, Peggy and John, were born in 1905 and 1907.

Gwalchmai's parents came from Cardiganshire to Cardiff in the 1850s and set up business building and repairing boats at Gabalfa Dock on the Glamorganshire Canal, which was at that time a busy waterway built to transport coal from Merthyr Tydfil to Cardiff. When Mary's diary opens, her father's six surviving siblings – two sisters and four brothers – are all still living close to the family's dock and their childhood home, Dock House.

The death of the eldest, Uncle Jack, in 1917, caused a family feud. Jack, unmarried and childless, left no will, so the question of who should occupy the dock and the house was the subject of bitter argument between his siblings. In any case, there appears to have been years of bad feeling prior to this, between Gwalchmai's sisters Polly and Ceinwen and their friend Mrs Bradley on the one hand, and Gwalchmai's wife, the fragile Hannah Candina, on the other.

Hannah Candina came from a farming family in Llanhilleth, Monmouthshire. Her mother died shortly after giving birth to her, and she and her three siblings were brought up by a housekeeper. When her father John died in 1895, she received a share in the farm, and perhaps more importantly, a share in the minerals beneath it. Despite the fact that she was seven years younger than her husband, the records show that she knocked three years off her age when they married in 1899 at a Presbyterian chapel in Pontypool, giving her age as 27 rather than 30. How the couple met is not known.

Although still involved in the boat business, Gwalchmai was mainly engaged in building streets of terraced housing in Llandaff North and Whitchurch, which he rented out: the names he gave them such as Andrews Road, Mary Street and John Street still bear witness to his activities. Collecting the rents fell to Mary and her sister Peggy from their mid-teens, and the horror of having to face the tenants and ensuring that the collected amount was correct down to the last penny to avoid Daddy's wrath, haunted Mary throughout her adolescence.

Gwalchmai used his wife's money to fund the business, and worked sporadically, never missing an opportunity to attend an Eisteddfod or the public meetings of Mr Lloyd George. Meanwhile he pleaded poverty, allowing his wife no help in the house. Mary, increasingly conscious of the strain in her parents' marriage, took up the slack on her mother's behalf, working hard at housework and feeling sorry for Hannah Candina in her 'quiet, cabbage life'; but she still hero-worshipped her ebullient father, whose political and musical enthusiasms she shared, and whom she accompanied on some of his jaunts.

When Mary begins her diary in 1916, her mother is not at home. On 10th August, Mary writes: 'Daddy left early to go to Bridgend to see Mother.' In fact, he was visiting her in Glamorgan Asylum, where she had been confined for a year. Her medical records state *she is in great mental distress, and very apprehensive: she is quite wrapped up in her own imaginary troubles: says she has ruined her husband and has been very wicked: complains she is unable to sleep or live at her home.'* The sole diagnosis is 'Climacteric' (menopause).

In the hospital, Hannah Candina made several attempts on her own life and was considered a difficult patient. But finally, in November 1916, she showed 'some definite improvement' and Gwalchmai brought her home.

It is against this background that Mary begins her diary, at the age of fourteen …

MAIN CHARACTERS IN MARY'S DIARY

MARY'S PARENTS

William Gwalchmai James (Daddy) b. 1861.

Hannah Candina James, née Andrews (Mother) b. 1869.

MARY'S SIBLINGS

Sarah Margaret James (Peggy) b. 1905.

John Andrew James (John) b. 1907.

THE JAMES FAMILY OF LLANDAFF (DADDY'S SIBLINGS)

Aunt Polly b. 1854. Unmarried.

Uncle Jack b. 1856. Unmarried. Dies 1917.

Uncle Davey b. 1858. Married to **Aunt Catherine** (d. 1917). Their only child, **Dorothy**, died aged 19 in 1914.

Aunt Ceinwen b. 1860. Married to **Uncle John** (Rees). One daughter, Ethel, b. 1897.

Uncle Ted b. 1869. Married to **Aunt Bessie**. One daughter, **Olwen** b. 1900 and one son, **Hughie** b. 1907.

THE ANDREWS FAMILY OF LLANHILLETH (MOTHER'S SIBLINGS)

Aunt Mary b. 1860. Married to **Uncle Adam** (Jones) of Penycoedcae. Four sons and three daughters, including **Elizabeth Ann** (Betty) who dies by drowning in 1918.

Uncle William b. 1863, of Hafod Arthen Isha. Married to **Aunt Rachel.**

Uncle Ted b. 1866, of Mount Pleasant. Married to **Aunt Polly** (not to be confused with Aunt Polly James). One son, **John** b. 1894, and two daughters, **Madge** b. 1895 and **Goleu** b. 1904.

NEIGHBOURS AND FRIENDS

The Ward Family. Neighbours at No. 51 Station Road. Valerie Ward is a playmate of Mary's brother John. Mary sneaks into their house to read their *Strand* magazines in an unusual act of mischief.

The Platt Family. Former neighbours at No. 53 Station Road. Mary and Winnie Platt are penfriends after the family moves away.

The Arthur Family. Dr Arthur, the family's doctor, originally from Ireland, lives nearby at Hilton Place with his family, including grandchildren Pat and Gracie Arthur, who annoy Mary when they come to play.

Miss Edmunds. A friend of Mary's mother, who lives at Aberbeeg, Monmouthshire, near to the Andrews relatives. Mary stays with her in 1918, and Uncle Davey considers marrying her, much to Mary's disapproval.

ENEMIES

Mrs Bradley a.k.a. 'The Old Dutch'. Friend of Aunt Polly James and Aunt Ceinwen, and aunt of Mary's friend Gladys Mees. Hated and feared by Mary and her mother, although we never find out why.

Miss John and Miss Celia John. Celia John is Uncle Davey's housekeeper, with matrimonial designs upon him, and her sister, Miss John of Creigau, is a 'vulgar, impudent old thing'.

YOUNG MEN IN MARY'S LIFE

Leonard Jotham. The green-eyed boy from Mary's first school whom she idolises until he loses his ideals and indulges in asinine behaviour.

James Hamilton. Mary's Scottish pen friend, whose letters she awaits in 1918.

CARDIFF HIGH SCHOOL

Miss Layton. A dedicated teacher whom Mary credited with improving her learning and behaviour, and whose approval she constantly sought.

Vera McConochie. A friend and fellow pupil in the sixth form with whom Mary has a bitter falling-out.

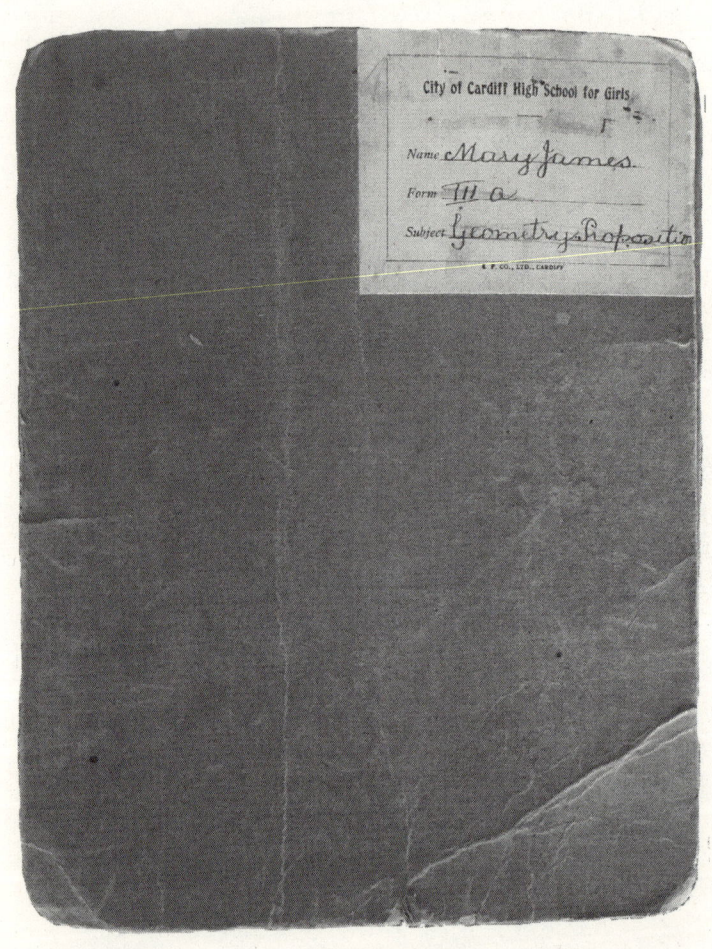

Front cover of Mary's first diary notebook

1916

I want to tell you of something I have been thinking ...

The first page of Mary's diary

MONDAY 7 AUGUST 1916

TO MY DIARY, greetings! My new diary. Do you know, I feel rather nervous about it? I have never kept a diary before, and I am not quite sure how to set about it. I shall confide a great deal of my secret thoughts and anxieties to you, because I know you will never, never disclose them.

But, to commence – today was the day when churches and chapels hold their Sunday School treats. About 5:30 the tea was announced, a bell rang, and the children ran up to the end of the field. There they seated themselves in rows, each with a mug in his or her hand. Ladies came round and poured out a queer-looking brew.

'Cake!' 'Cake!' 'Hurry up!' 'Hurrah!' I never heard such a row. One little boy shouted, to the great disgust of the ladies, 'Bread and scrape! This way!' Another child, of about four years old, passing her mug for more tea, exclaimed 'Hurry up! I've only 'ad eight cups!'

After their hunger had diminished a little, various cries of distress arose. One small maiden wailed, for the benefit of the company, 'Hi! Lily Jones 'as upset 'er tea, and I've bin and sat in it!'

Others went for mug after mug of tea, and conscientiously threw every one away. Some boys thought it would be best to save some for afterwards, so they crammed cake into their pockets. Altogether it was a very lively and amusing scene.

After tea we left the field and walked down to Uncle Jack's. There we found Auntie arrayed in shining black silk, for she, accompanied by Ethel, was going for a drive with

Aunt Catherine, towards Canton. Uncle Jack was mending, or trying to mend, his bicycle. We stayed a little while, then walked down to Uncle Davey's, where we had some apples, and walked in the garden.[1]

We reached Hafod Arthen on the stroke of eight, had our suppers, and went straight to bed, and I for one was not sorry to get there.[2]

TUESDAY 8 AUGUST 1916

AFTER BREAKFAST, I washed and wiped the crockery and arranged all the flowers. Now, at about 11, I am supposed to be sewing buttons on gloves, but have stopped to write. The milk has just come, brought by John. I don't know where he has got it from. I think he has drunk a little, but never mind.

I want to tell you of something I have been thinking. It's really very silly, but I have been reading a good many books lately in which the beautiful young heroine imagines herself in love with a handsome undesirable. Almost invariably the angry Papa banishes the young man, forbidding him from seeing his daughter any more. Now, isn't that the silliest thing he could possibly do? For, when he is away, she remembers only his virtues and forgets all his irritating faults. And she goes on worshipping, not the man as he really is, but a

[1] Uncle Jack lived at Dock House, Gabalfa, and Uncle Davey at College Farm.
[2] Both the houses on Station Road in which Mary lived were named Hafod Arthen, after her mother's family's farm in Monmouthshire.

creature of her own imagination, invested with all the hero's virtues and charms. If the young man was allowed to be with her frequently, in a month she would have completely tired of him; all his irritating manners would have been noticed by her, until they drove her nearly desperate. Of course, if her love was the real thing, not merely a girlish infatuation, she would love on still, in spite of his defects.

But to finish these musings. Today, directly after dinner, the children and I went down to Uncle Jack's. We passed a pleasant afternoon playing on the hay and talking to Auntie Polly. Then we had tea, and afterwards Mrs Bradley arrived. I departed and had a jolly time paddling. Soon I went into the hayfield, and employed myself in making cocks of hay until I was tired (which was not very long, I may tell you).

Afterwards I watched two little boys, Albert Stone and Lewis Stone, doing somersaults for my benefit. They are both so fat and podgy that they reminded me of Tweedledum and Tweedledee.

I talked for a time to Cissy Stone; she is a sensible and intelligent little girl, though rather given to running down her uncle and family. Her family is clean, honest and respectable, while her uncle's is the reverse, as the poor man is given to drink.

The lighting restrictions are now in force and are a great nuisance. We have to darken our bedroom windows; there is really no need for it, I am sure.

WEDNESDAY 9 AUGUST 1916

I SHALL WONDER, I know, when I read this diary in future days, that during the stupendous struggle that is going on practically all over the world, I should make no reference to it, and write of the small things with such zest.

But, my dear grown-up Mary, fourteen-year-old Mary wishes you to remember that the war, up to the present time, has never really touched me. Except for trifles, such as having less sugar in tea and porridge, less jam, using Blue Band instead of best butter[3], and other little economies, I have not felt the war at all; there might not be one on. It sounds dreadful, but it is true. It is not that I am callous; one cannot feel the same for others' woes as for my own. I have not shed a single tear on account solely of the war!

I am not complaining; I humbly thank God for being so much more merciful to me than he is to the great majority. The great push in the east, which the Russians are making; the great push in the west, which the British and French are making; the distresses on the Italian-Austrian frontier; the battle that has taken place near Port Said, in the howling desert, between the Turks and British: all these things I have heard of, but they are not distinct and sharply defined as alas they are to many, with me. They are all dreamlike and shadowy.

But enough. Each day I will pick some of the most important news from the paper and put them down here. It will be interesting, later.

[3] Blue Band: a brand of margarine

Today's war news – Two severe defeats, double blow for Austria, Brusiloff's push for Lemberg, 16-mile front broken – that is Blow Number One.

Blow Number Two, Italians at Gorizia's Gates, Austrians surprised. Hurry up Italia!

In the Salonika zone, the Franco-Serbian force defeats a Bulgarian battalion. But on the Western Front, things do not seem so cheerful. Peronne is in flames. The famous picture gallery, with its collection of English and French masters, was destroyed by four or five direct hits.

British front, more progress at Pozieres.

Around Suez, in the Katia district, our army is pursuing the Turks in the desert. The Turks, while retreating, suffered so terribly from thirst that they even drank their camels' blood!

To return to details that affect me – today Miss O'Brien came, and made me a green dress, and began a pink voile one for Peggy. She is tall and dark. I like her very much.

We were not able to go out today, at all.

THURSDAY 10 AUGUST 1916

WAR NEWS. General Lechitsky's onslaught on the Austrian right has developed into a big victory, in which 7,400 prisoners were taken. Bravo Russians!

British front. North-west of Pozieres we made further progress, gaining all our objectives.

Austro-Italian frontier. Italian troops have entered

21

Gorizia! Bravo Italia!

At daybreak this morning, naval aeroplanes bombarded an enemy airship shed at Evere, near Brussels.

What a tale of horrors, let me go back to the little peaceful details of my daily life.

Miss O'Brien came again this morning, she finished Peggy's best frock, and started two simple dresses for everyday use. We were unable to go out again, but Daddy left early to go to Bridgend to see Mother. The day passed slowly and drearily. About half past ten, Daddy returned. Dear Mother did not seem quite so well. Oh, Diary, isn't it dreadful? It makes me so miserable to think of the state the darling must be in. I must write to Maywen Mathias, her mother is just the same as mine was exactly a year ago. I am so sorry for the family.

SATURDAY 19 NOVEMBER 1916

IT WAS THE greatest mistake to put in war news. 'Interesting' indeed! I don't think! Reading this diary today, those are the parts I skipped, all along. Today we had snow on the ground all day. Early, isn't it?

Mary's mother, Hannah Candina,
as a young woman

Mary and Peggy, c.1907

1917

*One glorious thing has happened since I wrote last,
Mother has come home ...*

Gwalchmai and Hannah Candina James
with their children, c.1908

TUESDAY 6 MARCH 1917

LAST FRIDAY morning Doctor Arthur had a severe stroke, he is now very ill. Auntie Catherine is dead. It seems so terrible to me. The old familiar friends of my childhood are already failing. How sad it is!

But one glorious thing has happened since I wrote last, Mother has come home. How happy we are you can easily guess, dear Diary.

Springtime is here!

MONDAY 16 APRIL 1917

WE BROKE UP on Friday, our holidays are to last until May 1st. I am going to keep a diary of them.

Today nothing particular happened. I have been a good girl helping Mother nearly all the time. I couldn't do much else, it is a horrid, wild, wet and stormy day.

TUESDAY 17 APRIL 1917

TODAY WAS a lovely day, fine and sunny. We decided to visit Creigau, a little village set on a hill near Pentyrch, which is beyond Taff's Well. Daddy and I cycled to Gwaelod-y-Garth, where we were met by Mother and Peggy and John. They had taken the train to Taff's Well.

We then walked up the mountain. I pushed Daddy's bike and Peggy pushed mine. My, it was a walk. Always going up and up, and the view if you turned round! We were in the midst of gently undulating hills, all fertile, some crowned with woods, others with pasture. Above us was the glorious blue of the sky, and around us the lovely hills. At last, we crossed the brow of the hill and came upon Pentyrch, nestling on the other side. A quaint little place is Pentyrch. I like it very much; it is so pretty.

On the way to Creigau, we passed a beautiful house standing on the brow of a hill, lovely verdant meadows sloping from it. This beautiful house is the property of Mr Tom Evans. To the left of it stood a large farm, Pentwyn. The former farmer of Pentwyn was a man named John. When he died (his sons being in Africa) his two daughters and wife gave up the farm. One of them, Celia, came as housekeeper to my Uncle Davey. Then Mrs John died, and the other daughter bought a very small but dainty house in Creigau. Celia still stayed with Uncle Davey, in the capacity of housekeeper and I think she intends to stay, though perhaps not always as a mere housekeeper.

But it was her sister in Creigau that we wanted to see. At length we got there. Oh Lor'! She was a 'Bachelor Lady'! Stooping, spectacled, immensely clever and superior. Ugh, she did make me bristle!

Although we had brought our own bread and butter, she did not seem pleased at our numbers and when our small loaf was exhausted, offered us nothing more, but sat and bragged of her famous and wealthy relations and the glories of her former state. Ooh! She made me sick!

She was also intensely ecclesiastical. 'Mrs So and So, the Vicar's wife says that …' 'The Vicar said …' 'This jam was made by the Archdeacon's daughter …' 'The Dean and his wife came to tea yesterday' 'The vicar of Creigau likes this jam …' Oh! She was potty!

I was glad to get away. One crowning thing, she spoke of my uncle, Mr David C. James, as … what do you think …? 'James'! I couldn't think who she meant until I understood that 'James' meant Uncle Davey!

Vulgar, impudent old thing. Oh, my goodness me! Such specimens of old maids are enough to frighten a girl into marriage with anything!

WEDNESDAY 18 APRIL 1917

IN THE EVENING I did something which proves my moral courage, I think, that is I went to Gladys Mees. Just as I came up Theobald Road, the Old Dutch [Mrs Bradley] came down it. We met. Oh Lor'! I jabbered madly. She said she had dreamt of me. I nearly said, 'Thank you'!

Saw Gladys, the dear girl. She greeted me cordially, and I read her splendid testimonials. Had no unpleasantness, except that the Old Dutch kept looking out of the window, so I turned my back and talked to Gladys.

Gladys is very busy, so I went after about an hour. I was glad I had gone, to show there was no ill feeling towards the Mees.

How I hate Mrs Bradley! It is she who divides us. I wish

she would go far away somewhere.

THURSDAY 19 APRIL 1917

GRACIE ARTHUR came to tea in the afternoon, so we all went into Maplewood.[4] Gracie made us pull her along on John's trike, but we had a fairly decent time. Maplewood is beginning to look prettier now. The grass is spangled with daisies, the daffodils are showing their pretty heads, and the trees are bursting into bud.

We had a nice tea, and after it a quiet evening. I couldn't go into Maplewood because (I know it's silly) Grace and Peggy will have little boys in with them now, and I detest seeing girls cadging up to boys as they do. There are two brothers that they are fond of at present, Douglas and Cyril Morgan they are called. I think they are about twelve and ten respectively. They are fine, handsome boys, well grown and well dressed, you know.

FRIDAY 20 APRIL 1917

YOU KNOW I got a letter from Winnie Platt lately? We wrote to them some time ago and they replied. I thought it was jolly of them.

4   Maplewood was a house in large grounds on the other side of Station Road.

Winnie seems to have developed into a sporty sort of person, keen on games, spectacled, hates babies but likes boys, awfully clever and so on, you know the sort.

She is very tall and stoopy. I hope she will not develop into a second Miss John, not Celia, I don't mean. But I don't wish to be unfair. I expect she is a jolly sort of girl. Anyhow, I was very glad to hear from her.

SATURDAY 21 APRIL 1917

MORE HAPPENED TODAY. Good job, too, I don't like to feel that I am vegetating, do you? In the morning, I performed my usual duties. But in the afternoon, Daddy and I mounted our bikes and went for a ride. It was a very hot, sultry sort of day, you know the kind, a damp, dull sort of heat. I had Dorothy's mac on, and my dress was too untidy to take it off![5] I nearly melted! Honestly.

We made for Llanishen, pushed up a desperate hill and went to the bottom of the Cefn Coed mountain. The road was rising all the time – phew, it was fagging! At last, we turned back and came round past old Lisvane church. In Lisvane, of course, Uncle Ted has bought a house with a lot of ground and its back facing the road, which it is right on top of. I need not describe it further, because I dare say it will be there for all to see when I am gone. Outside we saw Uncle Ted's car, and Olwen saw us.

[5] The only reference in the diary to Mary's late cousin Dorothy, Uncle Davey's daughter.

Olwen, Auntie and Uncle had motored down from Porthcawl where they are staying. I was surprised to see them. The men for decorating had not arrived (they are having it all done up regardless, positively heedless, of expense) because there had been some dispute, and they cannot get possession until next Tuesday.

Olwen is mad! She was busy acting the silly ass. To my idea, she acts that part to perfection. She was busy picking daffodils, but she never told me to pick a few. Every now and again, she would affectedly smell them, shriek 'Exquisite!' and rush up and down, to the immense gratification of her adoring parents. I do not like her at all. She looked ever so nice, I thought, in a blue frieze coat and skirt, very nicely made, and a white Panama hat, which showed off her skin to perfection. She is really rather pretty, I think, with her golden hair and glorious complexion.

In the evening, I went to the library and got a book called *Daphne in Fitzroy Street*. It depicted a man so devoted to his work – artist, of course – that although he loved a simple, trustful girl, Daphne, he would have nothing to do with her, believing that she would interfere with his work. Eventually he came to realise his mistake and married her. But still, it was an unusual type of tale. If you only knew how tired I am of tales which bring a man and a woman on the scene, obviously meaning them to come together and then relate the manner of their coming. That is indeed a timeworn device, how tired I am of it.

SUNDAY 22 APRIL 1917

TODAY WAS JUST the same as Sundays usually are. Get up, breakfast, scurry and rush to chapel, go round the 'Long Way' across the canal bank, get to chapel, be bored (usually, at least I was today, awfully). Home again, wait for dinner, which is at last ready. Dinner over, lounge, (after having wiped loads of crockery), read library book, tea (for which one has no appetite), after tea go to chapel. The preacher was interesting, so was glad I had gone. Come back, supper, go to bed. So goodnight, Diary!

MONDAY 23 APRIL 1917

THIS MORNING AFTER the usual little jobs, Daddy asked me, me, me to *Collect The Rents!* Oh, me miserium! However, I collected the Whitchurch ones all right, trembling, hoping, praying that I would make no mistakes, that I would not lose any money, that the tenants would not cheat me, that I would give the right change, that they would not think me stupid because I was slow to reckon up the money, etc. But the ladies were very kind, and I tried to be pleasant and affable. In Whitchurch I got everything all right. But down the Freehold, I was scared, horribly shaky, to tell the truth. My fear was accentuated by the fact that in Whitchurch I had, in every rent book, put the date wrong; I put next Monday's, in fact. Oh horrors, but Daddy said it would be all right.

Down the Freehold, I was more careful and came back with the right money, but threepence over. I don't know how I got those extra pence. But I was glad it was that way and not the other.

TUESDAY 24 APRIL 1917

THIS MORNING I felt very fresh and happy somehow. After breakfast I helped Mother to wash up the crockery, then the washerwoman came. I went to Jones' the shop, and after that took a chrysanthemum plant down to Mrs Hobbey, an old tenant of Daddy's, and also called at Treseder's and bought 50 cauliflower plants for him.

After that I walked in the big garden we have, what used to be Bevan's patch. It is looking lovely now, the earth so rich and brown, the currant and gooseberry trees speckled with green, and the air of life about it all. Oh! It is lovely in gardens in the spring!

THURSDAY 5—FRIDAY 6 JULY 1917

THESE LAST TWO days I have passed through a strange experience. I do not know whether any other girl of my age has felt what I have.

You know how, for some time, I have been dreaming

dreams about a certain person.[6] I dreamt of him as strong, pure, and work-absorbed. Yesterday, this image was cut down at the roots. To speak plainly, I had the good (or bad) fortune to land myself in a carriage where there were seated several boys and some girls. Leonard Jotham and Cyrus Apjohn were there, together with Winnie Perrin, Rachel Denis and another girl, something Davies, and another, something Morgan. Then the row started. All the boys smoked and behaved rudely to the girls, who seemed to enjoy it. The more I think of it, the more disgusted I become. They were so very – vulgar! And Leonard Jotham was one of the most uproarious, the most free in his behaviour and altogether most asinine! It was a pretty severe shock to me, I can assure you.

At first, I was too disgusted and horrified to think clearly. I had already, with trembling, feverish hands torn the cherished image down from its accustomed place. But in bed last night, the 5th, a new and strange emotion almost overmastered me. I was filled with a kind of pity, almost, I could say, Mother love, but it seems so ridiculous to think about. The more I thought of it, the sadder I became. I could not sleep, I wept, I really did, for a boy to whom I have not spoken for three or four years.

I know that Leonard has brains, he used to be persevering and hardworking, honest and perfectly straight. I could kill those girls, those wicked girls who by their frivolity and coarseness, encourage boys to familiar intercourse with them.

6   Leonard Jotham who had been a fellow pupil at Mary's first school, Lockley's.

They suffer every rule of modesty to be ruthlessly torn down. How can one expect men to honour and respect women when they are allowed, by coarse girls such as these, to treat them with such vulgar freedom? I thought of Leonard losing his ideals through the baneful influence of these girls and again I wept. I felt like a mother of about 90, looking down on the follies and indiscretions of youth. How did I come to have this sort of age, I wonder? Do other girls of fourteen think as I do? I don't think so, somehow.

FRIDAY 27 JULY 1917

TODAY WE BROKE up. I came tenth in the term. We do not know the other results because we have taken the C.W.B. exams this year. With Mabel Roach, Rita Farrel and Elaine, I walked home through Llandaff fields.

SATURDAY 28 JULY 1917

I WAS DOING housework until about twelve, then washed, dressed decently, and went on my bike to Whitchurch. I went to the shoemaker's with my bag. Got home and after eating and washing up, we decided to go down to Uncle Davey's hayfield. Therefore Peggy, John, Gracie, Boyo Owen and I trotted down there. Boyo is a new discovery. He lives in Stretton's old house. He is a Roman Catholic. He is 13 years old and is absolutely tremendously big, not only tall, but also fat and broad. He is not at all handsome, his face is too heavy and swarthy. But he is a very nice boy. I like him because he is so considerate and courteous to girls. He treats them with much more respect than is usual now.

Arrived at the hayfield, we went up on to the rick. I knitted up there, the others paired off. John and Gracie played mad games in the hay, Peggy and Boyo chatted gaily, until Peggy tired of him and went off on a new sensation.

A little later, when we had gone down from the rick, Daddy had the misfortune to poke a boy with his pike. Oh! I was frightened for it bled like anything. I ran away down the field. But fortunately, it was not the boy's eye, but very near it. Afterwards, Boyo came up to me, quite concerned – 'Did it make you ill?' he said. I answered 'No!' though it did make me feel very horrid. I like a boy to be considerate and feeling like that.

SUNDAY 29 JULY 1917

TODAY WE WENT to Tabernacle in the morning, and Sunday School in the afternoon.[7] All very dull, of course. A man by the name of Mr Jones, a brother of Mrs Edgar James, was preaching. He is a terrible man. His aitches are very uncertain and his grammar doubtful. He introduced long words, of which he had not the faintest idea of their meaning,

[7] The family attended Tabernacle Calvinistic Methodist chapel in Merthyr Road, Whitchurch.

and the effect was sometimes startling, as for instance:

'Napoleon I, Judas and Herod the Great richly deserve the unqualified censor passed upon them by all ages ...' etc.

This is rather awful, you must admit – 'richly deserve the unqualified censor' – oh dear me!

MONDAY 30 JULY 1917

TODAY WE ALL went, that is Peggy, John, Gracie, Boyo and I, down to Uncle Jack's haymaking. We paddled in the brook, came back, and lounged in the hay. The rest caught butterflies, or tried to, and I read a book that Boyo had brought down, called *Richard Chatterton, V.C.* He said it was very nice, and from what I read, I think it is.

In the afternoon, we went down again to the hayfield and sat upon the rick. The boys there were calling out 'Hullo Mary!' Wasn't it awful? There was a pole stretched across the rick, and on this we did gymnastics. I was going to do some quiet unobtrusive ones and I had my hand on the boom when they shouted, 'One, two ...' and laughed when I fell back, blushing.

TUESDAY 31 JULY 1917

TODAY, I WORKED in the morning, having woken up with toothache, which got steadily worse as the day wore on.

However, we had arranged to go up to the Garth with Miss John, picking wimberries. We caught the 3:07 train from Llandaff, and having arrived at Taff's Well, we walked along until we came to the foot of the Garth. The country, hilly and picturesque, was often very beautiful. We had tea at a cottage half-way up the hill. We had brought our own food, and they gave us the hot water, table, etc. The house had a large verandah sort of affair, and from this one could see the hills all around. After tea we went along up the Garth and picked the wimberries on the very top. It was a wearisome job. I found a place where there were ever so many. That windfall helped me along, I can tell you.

My toothache by this time was simply ramping. There was a stiff breeze blowing, and my hair, which was loose, got very untidy. We then retraced our footsteps. Miss John led us. Poor old Johnnie, I know she hates us. One time we hid, and she started squalling out 'Mary! Peggy!' etc. Oh dear, she is a funny old stick. The country through which we passed was very pretty and old-fashioned in its appearance. We saw the nuts hanging on the hedges, and the ripening blackberries.

WEDNESDAY 1 AUGUST 1917

TODAY I STAYED in bed, I was miserable. The toothache was an absolute sin.

About the middle of the morning, Mother had a call on Doctor Arthur's telephone. Tremendous excitement ensued.

We were awfully flustered. I thought something must have happened to our relations in Monmouth. I got up and dressed, trembling so much that I could hardly stand. And after all, it was only Auntie Bessie asking how to make some chutney that Mother had the recipe for. Oh dear! Grand climax! I nearly collapsed when Mother, panting and furious, told me what she was wanted for. How thoughtless some people are!

THURSDAY 2 AUGUST 1917

TODAY IS JOHN'S birthday. He is ten years old. I was noticing what a pretty little boy he is. His head is perfectly shaped, small, like a little thoroughbred's. His forehead shows distinct braininess.

I stayed in bed until after brekker. I read *Freckles* and enjoyed it very much, but not as much as *Girl of the Limberlost*. Then I tried *At the Foot of the Rainbow* and did not like it at all.[8] I re-read parts of *Doctor Claudius*. Marion Crawford's style in this work gets on my nerves. I don't exactly know why. But I hate the way he has of assuming such knowledge of the customs of the 'Upper Ten' and aristocracy. I detest his manner of assuming that unless a man eats well and is handsome, he is worth nothing.

Well, the day passes very quietly, reading and writing, I do enjoy a day taken up with that sort of thing.

[8] All three books are by Gene Stratton-Porter, American author and naturalist, 1863-1924.

SUNDAY 5 AUGUST 1917

THIS MORNING Daddy, Peggy, John and I went to chapel. We had a special service, a form of Thanksgiving and Intercession celebrating the third anniversary of the outbreak of the war.

In the afternoon, at Sunday School, Mr Frank Jones gave a short lecture on the war. He spoke on 1) why we were glad we had entered the war and 2) why we were sorry. It was not so bad for an amateur.

In the evening, I pottered about. Mother and Daddy went to chapel, and I wrote to Winnie Platt at last, and to Elaine Bregeon. I feel glad I have done these duties now, and I hope to get some letters back soon. I love getting letters.

MONDAY 6 AUGUST 1917

I WENT INTO Maplewood after finishing my work. Played about there with Gracie, Bertie, Peggie, Gwyn and John. Gwyn suggested having a picnic tea in Maple. So we agreed to have one, just we six.

After dinner, I packed a basket of food, and everybody else brought food as well. All the afternoon we played together and had a lovely time. About half past four, we got hot water and made the tea. Then we laid all the food on the table and had share and share alike. It was awfully jolly. After tea we played again, then about half past seven we had supper by the cedar tree in another corner of the lawn. After supper we had a most lovely game of Outings and Innings. Then we went home, about nine o'clock. We had had a most lovely day, romping in the open air. Gwyn and Bertie were most agreeable, and we were such a lot that we could have heaps of nice games such as String Touch, Puss in the Corner, Dropping the Handkerchief, and Twos and Threes.

TUESDAY 7 AUGUST 1917

AFTER I HAD finished my domestic tasks, I went into Maplewood. The other five were already there. We arranged to form a sort of society, just we six. Then we decided to have another picnic tea and supper together. But alas! When I went in, I found that I had to go to the bank for Daddy. So, dressed in my second best white, and my black hat, I caught the half past two train. Town was just horrid. The usual Bank Holiday crowds and rough people from the Rhondda valleys.

THURSDAY 9 AUGUST 1917

TODAY WAS A most beautiful day. I was pining to be out. I got up at a decent hour and finished my housework quite early. Then I went to play with the rest of the society in Maplewood. We had some nice games and then went in to dinner.

After dinner, Mother arranged for Mr Woods, the

milkman, to take us for a drive in his governess car.[9] We went through Llanishen, past Uncle Ted's house, and instead of turning up by the old Lisvane church, we went across the hills to Penylan. We lost our way and went winding along narrow country roads for a long time, constantly bursting upon new views and scenery. It was perfectly lovely. Twice we saw the Channel, with the ships floating upon its gently heaving, sparkling breast.

I have never been quite that way before, so the scenery was quite new. It is a pity people do not study their own lovely countryside first, before going off to Switzerland and other places.

FRIDAY 10 AUGUST 1917

IN THE AFTERNOON, after dinner, Peggy, John and I walked down to the dock, to get some pears. We saw Auntie Polly and Auntie Ceinwen. They were both very pleasant, and we talked a while. After, we looked for some pears, but Ethel had had them all except a few. She is very greedy, it seems to me.

Ethel went with Miss Dessie Jordan to Llanwrtyd Wells today. I hope she will be sick after eating all those pears. I do not like her, after what I saw of her that Saturday I was in town with her. She said the Bank Manager winked at her! Disgusting!

---

[9] A small tub-shaped conveyance, pulled by a single horse.

SATURDAY 11 AUGUST 1917

TODAY I DID my hair a new way. Peggy scrapes it back, holds it back with a slide, and then plaits it with one plait. I look so funny, but when I go back to school, I am going to start plaiting my hair in one plait. I am 15 now, oh dear me!

However, this morning I had a lot of housework to do, as it was Saturday. I did not finish very early. Then I went into Maplewood for some flowers and got some lovely ones. Then I helped Peggy and Mother to drive the hen and her seven small chickens ('dikkos', Peggy calls them) from the garden into the lane. They have made a horrid mess of the garden. I don't like chickens at all.

SUNDAY 12 AUGUST 1917

THIS MORNING I went to chapel with Daddy, Peggy and John. We wore our black dresses and as we were a bit late, we went the 'Short Way'. We had a very good preacher at Tabernacle; he is very nervous, however. He is too nervous to enter a pulpit and preaches from the raised dais below.

In the evening, Mother, Peggy and I went to the cathedral. I love the service there and enjoyed it very much. We met Mrs Bradley and Gladys. Poor Gladys was quite miserable, she was absolutely afraid to speak because of the Old Dutch. Mrs Bradley got a very nice squashing from Mother. Poor Gladys! I wish she would come to tea one day and learn to know and love Mummy as she really is. Mother is always a little affected in public and she was a wee bit nervous under the Old Dutch's scrutiny. How I hate Mrs Bradley!

MONDAY 13 AUGUST 1917

WE HAD BREAKFAST early and were well started on our work before half past nine. I worked quite hard, then Daddy asked me to go to Whitchurch to collect the rents for him there. I had to walk, for my bike was punctured. I got there and collected the money all right. Daddy gave me sixpence for going. Wasn't it dear of him? I have now 1/3d. I have decided to buy one of Gene Stratton Porter's books.

I had such a lovely dream thought lately, it was that someone of the opposite sex sent me the whole set of the *Limberlost* books, accompanied by a very nice letter, begging me to accept the gift and pardon the impertinence of sending it anonymously. The anonymity, he assured me, was to save me from embarrassment. And it was signed 'One of your Admirers'. Doesn't it sound silly and conceited, but I love to think like that. I do so enjoy lying in bed thinking dream thoughts like this.

TUESDAY 14 AUGUST 1917

AFTER TEA MOTHER and I went up to Mrs Lewis, the dressmaker. On the way, we met Mrs Sam Arthur and talked a bit to her. We bought some fish and chips (chish and fips) at that little shop near Thomas's, next door to Mrs Hodgetts. When we were in the shop Doctor Arthur passed by and Mother pretended to be chatting with the 'chish and fips' lady. I was bound to laugh.

Daddy had been down to Canton to look for a nice pony. When we were in bed, he came home with the joyful news that he had bought a lovely little pony and a most beautiful set of harness with silver plating. Of course, we have not seen it yet. Now we are going to look about for a governess car to suit the pony.

WEDNESDAY 15 AUGUST 1917

MOTHER AND DADDY have bought a black governess car. Luckily, it suits the horse, and everything is now settled and paid for. Perhaps we will be able to have a drive on Saturday. Won't it be lovely? We are going to keep both pony and governess car down at the dock. I hope it will be fine now, so that we can go for drives.

THURSDAY 16 AUGUST 1917

I SPENT THE morning arranging the flowers and doing other household work. Then we had dinner. We had just finished eating, but the crockery was on the table, and we had not washed up, even, when I went to the door and there was Pat Arthur, who had come to tea with John. John got ready, and Peggy, and they waited for me because I had to help Mother to wash up. Then we all went out. We all went down to the dock to see our new horse and we thought they might be haymaking down there.

We saw our horse; he looked so frisky and strong that we were all frightened. After a bit I went up to him and gave him the sugar I had brought. Then I stroked his nose and tried to make friends with him. He was not at all restive with me. I called him by name and tried to get him to know my voice. Then we went down to the bottom field, which was in hay. They had cut it a long time ago, but the rain had come on, and they were not able to haul it. It is finer now, and I expect they will soon be taking it in.

Uncle Davey came to tea as well as Pat. Pat ate an enormous tea, I thought he was never going to stop. Uncle Davey was speaking about Miss Edmunds. He talks as if he seriously intends marrying her. I hope he is joking. They are so totally unsuited for each other. Miss Edmunds is so prim and ultra-ladylike and Uncle so free and easy, never thinking what other people think. He would drive her wild and she would irritate him to desperation.

After tea, Mother went down to the dock to see our new horse and John and I amused Pat by playing various games. Just as we were on the doorstep saying goodbye to Pat, Uncle Ted's motor rolled up to the door. Hughie came up and said he wanted water for the motor. Olwen and an aunt of hers, Auntie Sue, and a cousin were in the car. The cousin, Claudia, is a very pretty girl. Olwen looked so plain beside her. We talked a bit, not much, I felt disgusted with them. They only call to get water, not because they want to see us.

FRIDAY 17 AUGUST 1917

THIS MORNING I got up fairly early. I went into the big garden and picked some kidney beans. While I was there, Nanna – Timms' servant – asked me for some sweet peas.[10] Cheek, wasn't it?

Immediately after dinner, Pat and Gracie Arthur came to tea. Peggy went out to play, so I had to amuse Gracie in the house and garden. She is rather spoilt and willful, and I found her distinctly wearing. After tea Gracie seized my dear doll, Queenie. She made me go up in the attic and play house with her. It was horrid, because I had all the nasty parts of it. I was simply fagged by the time her mother came for her to go home. She wanted to take my doll home and was very cross when I would not give it to her. She worried me for it the whole time. Then she tried to get all our other toys, but I wouldn't give her anything. She is very pretty, but not a nice child at all.

[10] The Timms family lived at 49 Station Road, a house which the James family later occupied.

SATURDAY 18 AUGUST 1917

THIS MORNING DADDY had to go and get the governess cart from Norman's. He told us to meet him at 9:30 at Uncle Davey's. I had time to wipe up and slice some kidney beans. Then Peggy, John and I started out. We took Uncle Davey's horse down to Norman's, because ours has a sore, and cannot be used yet. We had to walk down to Canton, leading the horse. John rode most of the way. He was rather nervous. At length we got there. The car is black, with green stripes. It is very pretty, but a little too small for the horse.

We rode home in the governess car. We called for Mother and started off again. We went for a very nice little drive in the country, up round Whitchurch and Rhiwbina. The country looked fresh and lovely after the recent rains.

After dinner we went for another drive. We drove towards Penarth, but turned off and went to Sully. It was a most lovely drive. The country was lovely. There were no hills, only rolling fields. The hay has just been cut and the grass of these fields looks most beautifully green. Soon we saw the sea. It seemed to girdle the cornfields like a sparkling, grey blue serpent. We got into Sully. Peggy, John and I walked down to the sea. It was very windy, but we got some seaweed and pretty shells and stones.

MONDAY 20 AUGUST 1917

THIS MORNING I was up early. I pottered about a bit,

then walked to Whitchurch to collect the rents there. I collected one too few – wasn't it silly? – and Daddy was cross with me, too. I was very sorry.

TUESDAY 21 AUGUST 1917

A SERVANT GIRL, one of the Powells', came to help Mother, then Pat and Gracie Arthur came to the door. They evidently meant to come and play all the morning. But next Sunday is a Rally Sunday at Sunday School, and John and I are singing, and Peggy is reciting. As we are not used to the harmonium, we had arranged to go up and practice on the chapel harmonium that morning. When we got there Mrs. Stevens, the caretaker, let us in and we practised. I had to play. It was very strange, but I got on all right. Dorothy Protheroe came in while we were there, and she practised her hymn with us. We got on all right. The harmonium is nice to sing to.

Our governess car is too small for our horse. But there is another car for sale at Norman's, which is bigger. So Mother, after she had had a cup of tea, went down to see it. Then, when she was gone, I saw a copy of *The Imitation of Christ* on a little bookshelf. Just for curiosity, I took it up, and settled myself on the sofa. I had no intention of giving it any but the most cursory attention. I read for a solid two hours, never moving except to turn over the pages. I was absolutely fascinated. I had never thought to find embedded in its short cryptic sentences and quaintly turned phrases such a wealth of wisdom, such indisputable arguments, such knowledge of man and his idiosyncrasies.

Consider the following:

Who hath a greater combat than he that laboureth to overcome himself? This ought to be our endeavor, to conquer ourselves, and daily to wax stronger, and to make a further growth in holiness

True quietness of heart therefore is gotten by resisting our passions, not by obeying them

Endeavour to be patient in bearing with the defects and infirmities of others, of what soever they may be, for that thou thyself also hast many failings which must be borne with by others

Remember always thy end, and how that time lost never returns

Are not these perfections? I was astonished to find such gems and truth in the *De Imitatione Christi*.

A little time after, I heard Daddy come in from the dock. He brought a blanket in blue and white stripes that belonged to his great grandmother.

WEDNESDAY 22 AUGUST 1917

I WAS JUST starting to slice the kidney beans when Daddy came up to the door with the horse and the governess car.

We all drove down to Norman's. There we changed the car. We got a secondhand one, a nice car but it wanted doing up a bit.

Then we drove to Cardiff Docks. It was a bit nervy driving through town as our horse was rather fresh. We were all on pins, but we were not allowed to show any nervousness. Daddy gets very cross if we do. What a dull, murky, workmanlike old place Cardiff Docks is! Can anyone work up any sort of affection for its heavy somber squalidness? I suppose they can, those who know it well and have worked there all their lives and thought and planned ... yes, I suppose it is possible to love the old place.

We then drove into Cardiff. Mother went to do some shopping at Howell's. We waited outside and Mr Shail came up. We found that we had bought his governess car, which he had just sold to Mr Norman. Wasn't it funny?

THURSDAY 23 AUGUST 1917

I GLANCED AT the paper; I notice chiefly the following facts:

- That there has been an air raid on the Yorkshire coast. Zeppelins bombs, and one man was injured. A squadron of aeroplanes dropped bombs on Dover, Margate and Ramsgate. The total casualties were 11 killed, and 13 injured. Three of the great Gotha bombing aeroplanes were shot down, and five escorting scouts (and probably more) were brought down in a battle over the sea by our Dunkirk hydroplanes.

- That there is heavy fighting on the British front at Lens and east of Ypres.

- We have had great excitement this year about the Russian Revolution. The soldiers on the Russian front refused to fight, and Kerensky, the Prime Minister, had a difficult job.

- On the French front there is further progress on the Meuse River, they have now 6,716 prisoners.

- The Pope devised a Peace Note a little while ago, in favour of peace. The Germans in the Reichstag discussed it yesterday.

- The Italian offensive is going on well. There is an incessant battle, and several new successes have been gained.

- In Arabia, the Arabs are revolting against the Turks. The revolt was carefully planned, and daringly executed. The revolt is serious, it is spreading, and the Arabs are driving out the Turks.

- The threatened great railway strike has now passed over. The men wanted an eight-hour day and seemed determined to strike as they could not get it, despite the commands of the Government. But now they have made a settlement, according to Mr. Bromley, the men's secretary – 'The Government guarantees, which we have now in writing, are very valuable, and I am confident that our efforts, whilst not obtaining the eight-hour day at once, have brought it nearer by ten years …'

Daddy had not come home when we went to bed. I kept vigil for him. It grew later and later and still he did not return. I grew almost frantic. About half past eleven, I got up and lit the gas. Then I wandered about the landing.

I thought of my other great 'vigil', nearly a year ago. It was when Mother was away in Bridgend. Daddy had gone to see her. He didn't come home for ages. I nearly went mad, I think I was beating the pillow, saturated with my tears, frantic with fear. I called upon God in my agony. 'God, God!' I called, like that. When he came home, it was about one o'clock. I rushed down the stairs and hugged him. I shall never forget that night.

Tonight was not so bad. I found out afterwards that Daddy had gone to Cae Nicholas, Uncle Ted's house. He came home about 12 o'clock. Then I went to sleep quite comfortably.

SATURDAY 25 AUGUST 1917

I WORKED MUCH as usual in the early part of the morning. We had dinner quite early, and then went for a drive in our governess car. We went through Fairwater Road and then drove towards St. Fagans. We passed Mr Radcliffe's farm and went on towards a dear little place called Pendoylan. There is a lovely old church there, of grey stone. We went a little way up the tower, and then wandered round the graveyard. In the door of the church is a huge old lock, and a massive old-fashioned key belonging to it. Daddy mentioned that in Llanon (Cardiganshire), in the church there, the lock and the key were made by his grandfather, and they have his name stamped upon them.

When I got home, I went to the library for a book. Afterwards I had to go to town to get a pair of trousers for John from Howell's. There was not a train until five minutes past eight. Town was simply horrid. I was terrified. When I got to Howell's, the shop was shut. So I walked straight back to the station. I had to wait some time for a train. When I got home, Mother gave me a row. So I went to bed feeling jolly miserable.

How frightening it is in town on Saturday night! I just hate it.

SUNDAY 26 AUGUST 1917

RALLY SUNDAY! Oh dear me! I woke up in spasms of fright. We started early and splashed through the rain up to Tabernacle. I was fearfully nervous. Then all the people came in. I was third on the programme. I sang up as well as I could, though I was shaking so much that I could hardly hold the book. I sang *There is a Green Hill Far Away*, to a very pretty tune. I hope it sounded all right! Peggy said her recitation beautifully. She always does, dear little soul.

They forgot all about John's song, until Daddy stood up and reminded the Superintendent about it. So Donkey Boy sang his 'Luther's Cradle Hymn'. He sang it well, too.

Dorothy Protheroe made a hash of her song in one place, poor soul. Her voice seemed to be going all the time. I was very sorry for her.

MONDAY 27 AUGUST 1917

OH DEAR! I have been very naughty and silly! I have left off writing in my diary for this whole week, and now on Sunday evening I am trying to scribble something up. Isn't it dreadful?

Today, Monday, nothing much happened. After dinner I heard that I had to go to the bank for Daddy. The banks close at three o'clock, and there wasn't a train till nine minutes past three, so I went by bus. Rita Farrel was on the conveyance, but I was not speaking to her. There were two officers near me. It started to rain just as we passed through Whitchurch. A very old gentleman shouted and waved to the conductor when we were quite a long way from him, the man must have seen him, but he paid no attention and the bus rolled on. The poor old gentleman was left standing in the middle of the road, staring blankly after the receding bus. Whereat the two officers chuckled loudly. Brutes! I could have murdered the conductor, and those two grinning apes.

When I got to the bank it was shut. So I went round

the back way as Daddy had said. Round the handles of the swinging doors were leather bands, which were attached to the wall. I pushed the doors inwards. Of course, they would not open. So I walked away. Later I found that they opened outwards, towards you. But I can't see the sense of having the bands at all, if that was the case, can you?

TUESDAY 28 AUGUST 1917

I CAN'T REMEMBER a single thing concerning Tuesday, so nothing important can have happened, can it? But then, nothing exciting or important ever does happen in my life. I expect I shall think later that this is a silly little diary, chronicling the most absurd things, such as slicing kidney beans, washing up and going for drives. But I don't think I shall tempt Fate by asking for adventures and excitements. Something horrid and sad might happen, and I would rather have nothing than disagreeable happenings.

THURSDAY 30 AUGUST 1917

AFTER DINNER SOMEONE suggested going to Cardiff to a cinema. The big picture was *Romance of a Red Cross Nurse*. It was rather decent. My pleasure was rather marred by the fact that as we were sitting in the gallery, I could not see any printing. I am afraid I am horribly shortsighted.

Then came one of those comic plays. It was so utterly silly that I didn't look at it. I hate to see men and women, presumably sane, rational beings, making such fools of themselves. Then came a Charles Chaplin episode. This too was silly and not as funny as Charles Chaplin's plays sometimes are. He posed as Prime Minister in this particular play. Some Prime Minister! 'Some' is the popular expression now. I think it comes from America. It is constantly used by all classes, and you are always hearing such remarks as 'Some hat!' 'Some cheek!' 'Some face, what!' 'Some swank!' It's rather silly really, but sort of expressive.

We caught the six o'clock train home, buying some Turkish Delight on the way. I don't know when I have eaten a sweet before, not for ages. War economy, you know. Some economy!

FRIDAY 31 AUGUST 1917

AFTER DINNER WE arranged to go for a drive. Daddy brought the trap up to the door and we drove off. The governess car is very pretty and ever so comfortable. There is plenty of room for six in it. We drove through Ely, then along the country road until we came to a little village called Caerau. From Caerau we drove on until we came to a big white gate. We opened this and passed through, without asking permission or anything. That is rather Daddy's way. We were then in what they call Cwrtyralla Park. There is a narrow but quite good road running through it. On either side of us stretched level green pastures, most beautiful to see.

It was a strange and exhilarating sensation, driving through the fields in this manner. I wished we could have gone on for ever.

Is it not true that nothing venture, nothing have? You must venture to go in, before you can have the delight of driving through the beautiful place.

SUNDAY 2 SEPTEMBER 1917

THE SECOND of September! Oh dear, not much more of the holidays left. In the morning we all went to chapel. Mr Viner officiated and was as dull as usual. We had a ripping dinner and then rushed off to Sunday School. I was the only one in my class, so went to Mr Morgan's class. He was very dull too. None of the girls paid any attention, they talked quite loudly to each other. I looked at him all the time and tried to take an interest in what he was saying. Which is impossible. But I am rather sorry for him and like to appear attentive, not to hurt his feelings.

MONDAY 3 SEPTEMBER 1917

THIS MORNING, I had a severe tiff with Peggy and retired to the back bedroom. I locked myself in, in fact.

After a bit I decided to go into Ward's. This sounds very startling, but I have done it before, when they were on their holidays last year. I did not record it in my diary, though. I get in through a gap in the wall in the tank room, behind the tanks. I scrambled through, went down to the bookcase in the dining room, and got two *Strand* Magazines. Of course, I put them back again after I have read them.

When I came home, I sliced some marrows and cut them into small pieces to be made into chutney. We have had a monster marrow this year, it weighed over 34 lbs. Daddy is a very successful gardener. Bevan's patch is quite transformed as a result of his toil and labour.

I feel that the affairs of the James family just at present are too interesting to be passed over without any notice. I must tell you what has happened lately. Well – you know Uncle Jack died without making a will, so the remaining brothers, Davey, Ted and Daddy had to divide his estate. They appointed Uncle Ted as administrator. So he started on his work. He got the estate evaluated, and then the next thing was to divide it into five equal parts, for Auntie Ceinwen, Polly and Uncles Ted and Davey, and Daddy. This was not done without much storminess, you may be sure. Auntie Polly and Auntie Ceinwen thought they were to have it all and were most annoyed when they found out they couldn't.

It was early decided that Daddy was going to have the dock, and he went down there to work every day. He and Auntie Polly had tremendous tiffs. She would not give him any food and behaved in a most disgraceful, unsisterly and ungrateful manner. She ought to be grateful to him, because it was through his influence alone that she obtained £100 worth of War Loan, and he also gave her £40. But she treated him worse than any of the others.

One day Uncle Davey was going to have tea with her when she started boasting about the amicable relationship that used to exist between her and Uncle Jack. Uncle Davey could not stand it, he gave her a piece of his mind. He told her straight what he thought of her and the way she treated Uncle Jack. Then he pushed away his chair and walked out, he would not have tea with her.

Then the quarrels broke out worse than ever. The worm had turned, you see. Uncle Davey had refused to be bullied by Auntie Polly any more. Daddy stuck to his guns in spite of her, he would not yield another inch or penny. She acted in the most awful manner towards him, and Auntie Ceinwen (cunning Ceinwen) was most insulting. She said to Daddy, 'You have not consulted my husband at all.' Daddy said (he hates Uncle John and so do I), 'Your husband! He has nothing to do with it! It is none of his business!'

On September 1st Daddy entered into possession of the dock, the house and the field adjoining the house. Auntie Polly wanted to stay on at the dock, of course, but Daddy would not have that. He insists that she should go to live with Auntie Ceinwen; that is quite right, of course. But the Rees's do not want her.

Yesterday, she announced to Daddy that she had determined to go down to Davey's. He was irritating and awkward, but she supposed she would have to put up with him! Of all the cheek! We all thought that it would have to be Uncle Davey that would have to 'put up' with her. She is a cool customer, to be sure! When she made this arrangement, she had not even consulted Uncle Davey. Daddy told him this afternoon what she had said. It was the first time for him to hear of her 'arrangements'. Naturally, he was furious. He exclaimed that 'he wasn't going to have any of those old Bettys about his place'. For of course Auntie Polly would bring all her old pals, Mrs Bradley, the Georges, Ethel and Auntie Ceinwen.

I am glad that he has put his foot down and refused to have her. But we cannot be too sure yet. I wonder where she will go to, eventually. I hope it will be a long way from here.

When I was in the middle of writing this, exciting news came. Peggy had met Mabel Roach, who had told her that I had passed my C.W.B. Junior exam with four distinctions.

TUESDAY 4 SEPTEMBER 1917

THIS MORNING I went to town. I walked into the City Hall and found the book of the results of the C.W.B. examinations. I found that I had passed all right, with distinction in English Language and Literature, Scripture, History and French.

I was nearly off my head with delight when I proved the results to be true. It wasn't bad, was it?

WEDNESDAY 5 SEPTEMBER 1917

TODAY WE DROVE up to Monmouthshire. We had our own governess car and Uncle Davey's cob. We got there at half past five. We had tea at Hafod Arthen, with Auntie Rachel and Uncle William. Then we went up to Mount Pleasant and saw Uncle Ted, Auntie Polly, Madge and Goleu. John, who is now a Lieutenant, was home. He has just completed his training. It has improved him very much.

On Friday I went to stay with Miss Edmunds, while Daddy and John and Mother went home. I had rather a dull time with Miss Edmunds, Aberbeeg is a fearfully dull hole. Miss Edmunds was very, very kind to me. She is rather fidgety though, one night she got up and started walking about the house in the dark. She is very drowsy, too, she drops off to sleep in her chair while someone is talking to her.

MONDAY 17 SEPTEMBER 1917

ON SATURDAY, PEGGY started school. She is going to Howell's School now. I expect she will get on very nicely. Tomorrow I am starting school. Oh dear, oh dear, these pleasant holidays are over. This book is finished now, I am going to put it away to read over some time when I am old. Do you remember our picnics in Maplewood? What fun we used to have! How long ago it seems since we had them! I wish we could have the holidays all over again.

The James's Upper Dock and house,
Glamorganshire Canal at Gabalfa, c.1920

1918

I am here in my little sanctum, writing my diary …

"Maplewood," Llandaff.

To be offered for Sale by Auction on 11th AUGUST, 1904, by
Messrs. J. E. GUNN & SON.

Solicitor to Vendor—
J. H. WESTYR-EVANS, Esq.,
17, QUAY STREET, CARDIFF.

Auctioneers' Offices—
WESTGATE CHAMBERS,
CARDIFF.

Maplewood, the scene of 'my childhood's paradise and mystery'
(Glamorgan Archives DSA12/1633)

APRIL 1918

THERE HAVE BEEN so many changes around me of late. It seems sad and hurts me somehow.

To begin with, all Maplewood's trees have been cut down! Every single one of my dear, dear friends ruthlessly felled. It makes my heart ache to think that never more will I see them tall and dark against the winter sky, all the delicate tracery of the twigs clearly outlined, never more see them bursting into green in the joyous spring; never again gaze into their cool green depths when they are clothed with thick verdant foliage at midsummer!

Maplewood, my childhood's paradise and mystery is laid bare. The trees screened it, they lent it a certain subtle fascination. It looks bare, ugly, infinitely pathetic without them, to my unaccustomed eyes.

This spring seems full of sadness.

MONDAY 29 JULY 1918

WE BROKE UP on Friday, and I came home with Elaine by train. It was not as jolly as usual: to begin with, Elaine and Muriel Bregeon are leaving, and Mabel Roach's father died on Thursday. This cast a shade over our spirits, to speak grandiloquently but truly, all the same.

Well, I got home, and prepared the dinner, for Mother was ill. All over the weekend I was housekeeper-in-chief, and thus very busy.

About twelve o'clock Peggy and I went for a short spin on our bikes, along Quarry Road, up the Big Hill, and home behind the high fields. It was a most lovely morning, not a cloud in the blue of the sky, and the sun shining brightly. Such weather is what we have been longing for (but hardly expected to have) during the past week, when we had the most torrential downpours of rain. It fell both thickly and heavily, making one fear for the crops. Many fields have been ploughed up this year, and sown with wheat, rye or oats. For instance, Uncle Jack's (now Uncle Davey's) beautiful hay field, with the old tree in the centre. It is planted with oats, which seem to be coming on well. Almost everyone now has one or more allotments, which they cultivate carefully. As for us, we have the garden at the back and also 'Bevan's patch', which Daddy has fenced around, dug up, and planted with vegetables and fruit trees since May 1917.

We are now living at No. 49, which overlooks the garden, and the Timms have removed to Whitchurch. We like it ever so much better at No. 49, there is more room, for one thing, so that we have been able to buy a billiard table, and convert the dining room into a billiard room, Daddy has great fun out of it.

Family affairs have changed somewhat since last summer; to begin with, we are on unfriendly terms with almost all our relatives. Uncle Davey we have no truck with, he has behaved abominably – cutting down the pear trees at the dock, and not letting Daddy have the field which he promised him. Therefore, we have nowhere to keep a horse, and cannot go for the lovely rides in the governess car which we enjoyed last summer.

Auntie Polly lives with Uncle Davey and Miss John, she is as horrid as ever. Aunt Ceinwen we never see, she is very sly, I sometimes think I hate her more than Aunt Mary. We are an amiable family, aren't we?

With regard to my own personal affairs, something exciting has happened to me. I answered an advertisement for a pen friend in the 'Quiver'. I got a reply, it was from a Scottish schoolboy, James Hamilton, who lives in Motherwell, Lanarkshire. He is a very jolly boy, I like him very much, and we are good friends. In future you will understand who I mean when I mention 'Jim', will you not, Diary dear?

Let me see, where was I, before I commenced all this preamble? Oh, I know, spinning on my bike with Peggy. Well, we came home, after an enjoyable little ride, and got dinner ready. I idled about until four o'clock, then I got ready to go to town, to get Daddy some 'torpedo loaves'[11], since he cannot digest our war bread. It is rather awful, I must say. Mother came with me to town, we did what business we had to, and then came home as soon as possible. For the rest of the evening, I did practically nothing, only strummed on the piano, and tried to sing, and then wrote a letter to Jim, in reply to his last very jolly one.

TUESDAY 30 JULY 1918

YESTERDAY'S ENTRY CLEARED the ground – didn't

[11] French-style baguettes.

it? – so I need not be so lengthy today. Well, I got up at seven, with a sigh. In the middle of my toilet (how swanky that sounds!) I got a letter from Winnie Platt. It was a very jolly, utterly frivolous and silly letter. After brekker, I tidied and dusted our bedroom, the billiard room and the breakfast room, which certain members of my family call the 'lounge'. This I will never stoop to, much to Mother's annoyance.

After that I came out in the garden, and sitting in the shade of the big apple tree, I am writing this. John and Peggy have been blowing bubbles. Now, however, Peggy has disappeared, and John sits on the wall, alternately eating apples and conversing with Valerie, whom he addresses as 'Ward' or 'Wardie', so you see there is nothing – er – lover-like in his attentions, oh dear me no!

I have a lot to do, really, only I do not feel like doing it. For one thing, I have a lot of reading to do these holidays: Dickens, Thackeray and other novelists, and all Shakespeare's plays. That's what I ought to be doing, only I am not. But this minute, as soon as I have finished this, I am going to get Dickens' *Bleak House*. O dreary shades of Jarndyce and Jarndyce, at least the first chapter is dreary. So farewell, for now, dear Diary.

(Later) Alas, I have not kept my promise to myself! I have not read my poor Dickens! Instead, after dinner, I messed about, and read Ethel M. Dell's *The Way of an Eagle*.

WEDNESDAY 31 JULY 1918

AFTER BREKKER, I helped Mother to wash up, swept and tidied the conservatory, and made my bed. Now I am sitting in the little tank room, where I worked so hard a few weeks ago. I want to read a lot of Dickens today, I really must! And my poor King John! So, goodbye for now, Diary!

Alas for Dickens and King John! After we had dinner, I helped Mother to wash up, and then Peggy and Valerie and I went for a little picnic in the high fields. We had tea on a little hillock, under the shade of an oak tree. Afterwards we read a bit and messed about.

I have had a jolly day, Diary dear, but I am so lazy. I have not done a thing to help me next year. I really must stop lazing so much, and start a serious course of reading, but I keep putting it off, and the tomorrow when I shall plunge into Jarndyce and Jarndyce has not yet come, but it must come – tomorrow. Ah well, we shall see!

THURSDAY 1 AUGUST 1918

AT HALF PAST seven, Peggy, Valerie and I were on the road walking towards Treseder's gardens. We strolled in these, among the plants and flowers, until about eight o'clock. It was cool and fresh out of doors; the sun was often shaded by clouds. Mother and I cleaned the attic, which we use as our storeroom for vegetables from the garden, and that done, I picked raspberries and otherwise pottered about until half past eleven. Now I am here in my little sanctum, writing my diary.

We had dinner at one o'clock. Then I came upstairs to my little sanctum and elaborated and formed a fragment which I had already sketched out – *The Cloud*. The idea came to me a week last Tuesday. I was watching a cloud rise from behind some trees, and gradually float over our house. Then I thought what the effect of a gigantic cloud rising from the horizon of a rolling moorland would be. It is a good subject, almost worthy of De Quincey, but the devil is to put it down, you want enormous descriptive power and word magic to convey to the reader the picture of the sunset moorland, then the cloud floating over, and above all, the effect on a solitary person. It is so difficult, without genius, to find words to embody the things of the spirit.

FRIDAY 2 AUGUST 1918

I WOKE UP this morning to the music of the rain spattering on the windows and the glass of the conservatory. It is John's birthday, and the poor child is in bed with a cold and general indisposition. He usually has a warm sunny day for his birthday, but this one is cool, wet and dreary, like an autumn day. I don't mind, however; I have a lot of reading to do, and do not want to be tempted out of doors.

We had dinner, after which I cleaned the knives and went up to Hoffman's for some cakes and cigarettes. I dressed for tea when I got home, and then laid the table very nicely, because Alec Sprudd, an old employee of Daddy's, was coming to tea.

Alec joined the army in 1914, soon after war was declared; he has been in the Dardanelles, in Mesopotamia, and in France. His service in Syria has made him very brown. He is a very nice boy, very cheerful and courageous. He has a great belief in Lord Kitchener, he thinks that if the Earl had lived, the present situation would not be as it is. I really believe that Kitchener of Khartoum was a great soldier, with a genius for organization. He never had a great opportunity to show what he could do. I remember the day when I heard of his passing. It was a cold, wet day, Muriel Bregeon and I were on the station platform, waiting for the half past four train. I saw on the placards – 'Lord Kitchener drowned!' It was so sudden and unexpected; it gave me a very real shock.

SATURDAY 3 AUGUST 1918

AFTER WE HAD breakfast, Mother went to town, leaving the household work divided between Peggy and me. Peggy and I soon quarreled, and she was like a little – well, I can't describe it! – all the morning. We are still in bitter enmity. I have finished my work for the morning and have come here to my little sanctum to write in my diary, and to read. I have resolved to read until dinner time, Diary dear, and you see if I don't keep my resolve!

First, I must make a brief note on the war news, it looks very promising. General Foch has captured a large town called

Soissons and is continuing a brisk offensive. The Germans are in full retreat, and the Marne Pocket is being closed. Some predict that this offensive of Foch's is the turning point of the war, we must all realise how much we have to be thankful for.

Still, only this week there have been threats of striking, and actual strikes in the munition works at Coventry, Birmingham, and other towns, and the attitude of the leaders of the South Wales miners leaves much to be desired from a patriotic point of view. Also, it seems somewhat late in the day to bring in a forcible Aliens Act, doesn't it? Most people think, and rightly, that precautions against aliens should have been taken in the early days of the war.

Alas! I have not touched dear Jarndyce, but it was not entirely my fault this time, for after dinner Daddy asked me to cycle with him to Lisvane. We wanted to look for a house there, called 'The Meadows', which is to be sold shortly. We had a delightful run through Llanishen. As we rode, we were getting nearer and nearer to the hills, which soon lay before us, not as blue shapes in the distance, but green and smiling, little white homesteads or tents dotted among the fields here and there.

So we rode on towards the hills and found 'The Meadows' to be a house rather delightfully situated on the road which runs to the base of the Cefn Onn mountain. We walked around the house, which was rather rambling, and somewhat untidy. But the view of the country around was lovely.

After tea, I had to go on several messages and shopping expeditions for Mother. Also, I wrote a letter to Winnie Platt, and posted it. I hope she will reply soon. I also want to hear from Jim.

Daddy has given John a new book, a boys' school tale called 'Playing the Game!' I have started it and want to finish it tonight. It is a very decent book; the characters are better drawn than is usual in books of this type.

SUNDAY 4 AUGUST 1918

THE FOURTH ANNIVERSARY of the war! You cannot help feeling a thrill when you think of what today means, or rather what this day in 1914 meant. Oh dear! What the world has suffered since that historic date! But enough of these trite moralisings. I am afraid I am somewhat like my namesake, Mary Bennet in *Pride and Prejudice*.

We went to chapel this morning, that is Peggy, Daddy and me. This year we had no special form of service, except that after a very poor sermon, Mr Viner asked Mr John Davies and Daddy to offer short prayers. Daddy got on all right, but he was somewhat nervous because Aunt Polly was present. She is a very wicked unnatural woman; she tries to poison everyone's mind against us by wicked slanders and to embitter our lives in every way. When I think of the way in which she has treated poor Mother, I feel I could kill her without any compunction. And Mrs Bradley, that unspeakably filthy worm! But I would have to hire someone to kill Elizabeth Bradley. I could not touch her myself.

It is most unfortunate that Aunt Polly should leave Aunt Ceinwen's (with whom she has quarreled) and come and live with my uncle 'The Professor', for now she can come to the chapel and make things very disagreeable for us there.

By the way, Uncle David got his title of 'Professor' by a remark of his to the effect that 'Well, we are all professors' (of the Christian religion). And a 'professor' he is, merely! Another title is 'Mr Pay-Tidy'. This term he applied to himself, and since he is the absolute antithesis of this, we continue to use the term in sarcasm. Mr John Rees Evans is a distant relation who is shirking service in the Merchant Service, in which he is a captain. Because of his fear of submarines, and his utter cowardice, we call him the 'Shirker'. The angular and ecclesiastical Miss John completes the amiable party now living in Uncle David's house.

After tea, I washed up, and Mother and Daddy went to the cathedral. I think it was because Aunt Polly will be in chapel, and Mother cannot take communion with her, she says she hates and fears her too much. Daddy is also going to request that he may not be asked to pray publicly while Aunt is there. Uncle Jack, because of the slanders the same lady had spread about him in the chapel, was obliged to refuse to do anything publicly in the chapel. Is it not wicked of that diabolical old woman?

MONDAY 5 AUGUST 1918

THE SECOND WEEK of the holidays begun! Oh dear! How time does fly!

I have read the first chapter of Jarndyce and Jarndyce or *Bleak House*. Congratulate me, Diary dear! I must continue it now. So good-bye for the present, I hope to read until dinner time.

I have read nearly all the second chapter! After I had done so, I laid dinner. Dinner over, Daddy asked to have tea at four o'clock so that he and I might go for a ride on our bikes. So, until four o'clock, I merely pottered around and read a weird book called *The Cruciform Mark*. It is rather a creepy mystery tale.

After tea, Daddy and I rode to Roath Park, and went to the open-air concert which is being held there this week. But alas! It commenced to rain, and all the people in front of us put up their umbrellas, so that we could not see anything. Wasn't it horrid? Daddy protested loudly and made everyone around us laugh like anything. Some people lowered their gamps as a result, but the majority stayed up. So, as our view of the stage was entirely blocked and the songs were not worth listening to, Daddy and I went.

TUESDAY 6 AUGUST 1918

THIS MORNING I was lazy. I could hear the rain coming down in torrents and lay drowsily thinking of something that pleased me. I am always making up stories to myself, then I think about them before I go to sleep at night, and when I wake up in the morning sometimes, I write them down, oftener not.

For example, all the 'Gordon Lennard' episodes are planned in these times, and afterwards written carelessly down. Gordon Lennard, you know, was invented to supply the need and longing I felt for a boyfriend. I honestly did feel the longing very deeply, Diary dear, and as I could not make friends with a real boy, I had to invent one. And I must say that he filled the gap fairly well: he was very real to me, he and his sufferings. Then, still urged by the same longing, I answered Jim's advertisement in the 'Quiver'.

You know what happened: he wrote back, quite politely, but refusing my offer of friendship. I was hurt to the soul, and very, very angry. You see, my pride is rather sensitive, and it was severely wounded. I composed a letter to send back to him; it was not indignant, but icily icy. Then, something told me not to send it. I waited. Then, about two days afterwards came Jim's letter revoking his first one. At first, I thought of returning it, then my pride grew easier under the balm of his revocation. I replied, and thus began the correspondence, which has given me, and I hope him also, very much pleasure.

One thing I must add: when the hurt was worst, I cried out 'Oh! Gordon Lennard, Gordon Lennard!' and added to myself 'You would never have treated me like this!' Then I began comparing Gordon Lennard to James Hamilton, unfavourably to the latter, I am afraid. This will show you, Diary dear, how real Lennard was to me. Now, however, he has faded and almost gone. In comparison to the living, real boy he appears (dare I say it?) unreal, almost ridiculous. So I dream no more 'Gordon Lennard' episodes, and it is unmaidenly to dream of a real boy, is it not? (Does that sound old-fashioned and maiden-auntified?)

I have been reading tonight's *Echo,* and something I have read there has made me feel absolutely sick with horror: the

Germans have sunk a hospital ship in the Channel, and as a result over one hundred people have perished. The majority of these were men who were wounded and lying on their cots, unable to save themselves. Think of those poor men, lying helpless and suffering, being precipitated into the cold hungry sea, and drowned! It cannot bear thinking of! Oh, those Germans, those diabolical beasts! How could they perpetrate such a deed?

WEDNESDAY 7 AUGUST 1918

AFTER TEA, I went down to Blosse Road Dairy, and chatted a while with Mrs Woods, our milkman's wife. She told me her little boy is going to the Boy's Intermediate at Cardiff. This will be rather a blow to Gwyn Tuckett, I am afraid, because he so desires that only aristocratic boys should go there. But if all except the sons of the gentry were excluded from the school, he himself, in spite of all his silly snobbery, would be the first to be rejected. Poor Gwyn! I can only hope he will wax wiser with increasing years. Pride, by which I mean an honest respect for yourself (not your birth, or your position or your wealth) is a solid virtue, which every man should endeavor to cultivate; but snobbery is of all things one of the most abominable.

THURSDAY 8 AUGUST 1918

DADDY HAD ARRANGED to leave Llandaff about quarter past seven for Neath this morning, so that I was up early. Daddy made a hasty breakfast and cycled to the G.W.R. station: he is going to the Eisteddfod at Neath and hopes to see Mr Lloyd George there.

In a moment I must begin a letter to our relations at Penycoedcae Farm, for we have had sad news of them this morning: my cousin Betty drowned yesterday in the River Usk, near Brecon. She was in training with a company of Girl Guides, and while bathing was seen to sink, and was drowned. Her body has been recovered. It is very sad, she was such a pretty girl, and very clever, too. She had adopted school teaching as a profession. Poor Aunt Mary! She is not very well and is also anxious about my cousins in the Army and Navy. We have written to her, assuring her of our sympathy. The sad happening has quite thrown a shade over us all, it was so tragic.

Well, it has gone four o'clock, and Peggy and I have to go to town this evening, to get butter. Howell's have not sent us any, and we are in a greaseless state. Rationing is a bother; but I suppose it is the fairest way of dividing the nation's food at times such as the present, when supplies are restricted. We have a great deal to thank Lord Rhondda for. It seems sad that he should die before he had put into operation his plans for 'saving child life', but he worked very hard at the Food Office, and did great work there. Undoubtedly the nation is in his debt.

Alas, Peggy and I caught the 5:25 train into town, and rushed to Howell's Stores, only to find that there was no butter in the shop. I have almost forgotten the taste of the commodity. Sad, isn't it?

We strolled around town for a bit, (a thing I loathe with my whole heart: and to make it worse, Peggy wanted to look at the shops, and I wanted to walk quickly and look at the people) and met Kathleen Proctor. She was dressed in deep mourning; I suppose they have given up all hope of Mr Jack Proctor (her brother) being alive. I am so sorry for them, because they have other troubles as well – the youngest little boy is deaf and dumb and helpless, while the father is in the North Sea, minesweeping.

Somehow, everyone seems to have trouble of some kind or another nowadays. I suppose that the war is responsible for the greater part. Everyone is praying for the end.

FRIDAY 9 AUGUST 1918

I HAD A disappointment when the post came: there was no letter from Jim, and it is quite time that one came. When he does not write at once, I can't help wondering whether he likes me any more, or has tired of the correspondence. Isn't it silly, Diary dear?

I pottered around until we had dinner, a very nice one, I must not forget to mention. Good dinners are not as usual as they once were.

Well, Peg and I went down for milk, and when I came

back, I went upstairs to talk to John, who is still suffering from acute toothache. I think I must have been 'hysterical', for I was saying the maddest things to him, making him laugh until his tooth began to ache again. So I thought I had better leave him, especially as he was getting rather nasty about it.

When I got down, Peggy told me that one of our little chickens had been run over by a motor car. The poor little thing's leg was broken, and the officer whose car had run him over, brought him in to Peggy. He was very kind, for he bandaged the chicken's leg, and told Peg to put it in the oven to keep warm. He said he would come again on Sunday to see how the little thing was. He seems to have been a very nice gentleman. The poor 'dikko' has now died; I am sorry – he was a pretty little thing.

SATURDAY 10 AUGUST 1918

I GOT UP about seven o'clock, having heard Daddy go downstairs. The dear man came home last night at some unearthly hour. The post came, but brought nothing for me; never mind, I expect Jim's busy, or something. I was cheered by finding that John was much better. I am very glad; it is so miserable to see anyone suffering and not to be able to do anything to help them.

Well, we had brekker about half past eight, but before that I had strolled in our big garden. It was lovely there, in the fresh morning air. The sun was shining from a cloudlessly blue sky, making the dewdrops scintillate and sparkle with all the colours of the rainbow. I noticed also what glorious colours are in cabbages. There is always beauty even in what we are accustomed to think of as the most commonplace and prosaic works of Nature: God is too great an artist to fashion anything without beauty.

The paper today is practically all taken up with reports of the Eisteddfod at Neath, to which Mr Lloyd George went, and which was a record success. Daddy enjoyed it very much, particularly the Cymanfu Ganu, or hymn singing festival which followed. Daddy said the thousands present sang the soul-stirring old Welsh hymns in a way he could never forget.

I washed up and pottered around until tea. Then Mother and I had to go to town. It was just miserable in town: the usual Saturday night crowds. I walked like one in a nightmare. When we got home, I was very tired and soon went to bed. Still nothing from Jim; I wonder why?

SUNDAY 11 AUGUST 1918

DADDY, PEGGY and I went to chapel along the 'Short Way'. We cannot ever go by the 'Long Way', because of Aunt Polly passing that way too. As it happened, she was at chapel. We had a very ordinary preacher; his name is Mr Thomas. When I was small, he once gave me sixpence, which was an unusual exhibition of generosity in a Nonconformist preacher (so Mother tells me).

Daddy asked me to ride with him to Aunt Ceinwen's, so

we set out on our bikes. Aunt has been ill, and still appears unwell; Ethel is the same as ever, and so is Uncle John. He is what I call a 'drawing room politician'; there are numbers of them about, and the war has brought them out. Uncle discusses political questions, the war, social affairs – everything, as one that speaks 'with authority'. He advises President Wilson, gives hints to Mr Lloyd George and argues at great length and upon unsound foundations. It would be very boring to listen to if it were not so amusing.

I was careful not to speak of anyone, Uncle David and Aunt Polly in particular, to Ethel, although she tried to draw me several times. She is a most unreliable confidante, for she repeats what you say with her own elaborations. I do not greatly care for her: she seems to me light-minded and frivolous, as well as ignorant.

MONDAY 12 AUGUST 1918

THIS MORNING DADDY and Mother were to go to Penycoedcae, to be present at poor Betty Jones' funeral. So I got up quite early, and after brekker Mother and Daddy left, taking with them a lovely little white cross of flowers from Peggy and John and I. Daddy had said that Peg and I had to collect the rents, so Peggy went up to Whitchurch, while I stayed with John, whom we could not leave alone. When Peggy returned, I went down to the Freehold. I was horribly nervous, but I managed to muddle through somehow. The most trying job was with Mrs Maloney, who lives in

Andrews Road. She will not pay her rent properly; and there is really no excuse for her, because she has plenty of money, but she is a perfectly awful waster. She talked to me like a flood, I could not stop the stream of words. Then she took me to see her sick child, a poor white wasted little thing, infinitely pitiful. I don't think the mother gives the little girl sufficient nourishment. Mrs Maloney ought to be ashamed of herself, because she gets an extra allowance from the Parish to provide for the child.

I have not had a letter from Jim yet, Diary dear. I can't help feeling rather anxious about it.

TUESDAY 13 AUGUST 1918

OH, DIARY, Diary, Diary! It is Friday afternoon, and I have not written in you since Monday. And recapitulation is such a weary job!

On Wednesday morning Peggy's officer called. He is a very pleasant gentleman, not exactly handsome, but he has a nice face, and a very cultured voice. His name is Captain Tibbles, he is an officer in the New Army. And that is the only exciting kind of thing that has happened, I think.

Oh, stay! On Tuesday, Peggy, John and I went to the cinema and saw one quite decent picture, called *The Hostage*. There was one 'animated cartoon' which purported to be a representation of the famous raids on Zeebrugge and Ostend, in the spring. They were quite a failure, in my opinion; I could imagine the scenes much better. That is why I loathe pictures in books of fiction; as you read, if the description is at all clear, you cannot help forming a picture in your own mind. Then to look at another's picture (not nearly so nice as yours, of course) is, to say the least of it, disconcerting and upsetting.

Now, I have something to tell you, Diary dear, I can't hide it any longer: I am getting anxious about Jim; you see he has not written since July 22nd, and I have written twice since then. What could be the matter, I wonder? I can't believe he has tired of the friendship – his last letter was so jolly and cordial! Yet it is a long time since July 22nd. He can't have been pretending all the time, and now become tired of it. If he has – oh Diary dear, what shall I do? But I can't believe that; his letters always seem so sincere. Perhaps he is ill, or in trouble: perhaps his family is in trouble, his father or mother dead; I hope none of these things are true, but it is selfish to prefer that they should be, rather than – the other thing?

SUNDAY 18 AUGUST 1918

'AND JOY CAME with the morning'! Oh, Diary dear! I was right in trusting and hoping. I had a letter from Jim this morning which explained his silence; he has had influenza; he is not tired of me! Aren't you glad for me, Diary dear?

I know you are. You are such a sympathetic soul: my Father Confessor, as the gentleman of 27 is to Hilda Davies. I was surprised to learn, on receiving a letter from her on Saturday, that she has a gentleman friend, who, in return for her being 'pals' with him, educates and encourages her to love literature, to read 'good' books and to love Nature. She is very fond of him and tells him everything; she says that what she owes to him is boundless.

I have never had any kind of 'Confessor' except you, Diary dear; neither have I had any encouragement, outside school, to take an interest in Literature or to become a Nature-lover; yet I love Literature and Nature very sincerely and, I believe, deeply. The atmosphere of my home is not, and never has been, in the least literary or artistic. I have no elder sisters or brothers to educate me or encourage me to take an interest in anything of that kind; and certainly, my parents have not. My tastes have been grown, cultivated, and cared for by myself.

Well, I must go on to describe the day: about quarter to ten we started for chapel, by the 'Short Way'. When the preacher came in, John was seized with the giggles, for he was very short and slight, with a place face, and his hair, very thick and dark brown, stuck out above his head for about six inches. I thought it was dressed so as to give him height and told Peggy so. He is a scholarly little man, I should think, judging from his sermon, which was quite good.

When we got home, we had a ripping dinner, really an excellent one. After it, Peggy, John and I had to trudge in the sunshine to Sunday School. There, my class had to go into Mr Morgan's. I was rather bored; Mr Morgan's voice is so sleepy, and he cannot make the lesson interesting, somehow. But I have to give earnest attention, in order not to hurt his feelings. I may say I am the only one there who does; the rest keep up a running fire of laughter and talk, regardless of his mild remonstrances. I feel so sorry for him, and long to shake those unmannerly girls; it is so mean to take advantage of the good man's mildness.

MONDAY 19 AUGUST 1918

OH, DIARY DEAR, Monday once more! How the holidays seem to fly! Well, I got up early this morning, went downstairs, and after brekker did the usual household work, besides writing to Miss Edmunds, and to Auntie Rachel, Hafod Arthen.

After I had written these letters, I had to collect the rents, a ghastly business, which I abhor. It is immensely wearing and tiring: the people standing gossiping at their doors always seem to regard me hostilely, the children stare, and I am so worried fearing I will give the wrong change, go to the wrong house, or lose a pound or so. I started about eleven, and finished about half past one, when I was thoroughly tired. I was sixpence short at the end of it. I was afraid to tell Daddy (aren't I a miserable coward?) and made it up out of my own money.

The only time I enjoyed myself at all this morning was when I was walking down to the Dock House, along the canal bank. The land on the right belongs to the Marquis of Bute and is very beautiful. There is one large field, whose grass is a most freshly vivid green, cropped close like a lawn by the cows who browse over it. It is almost surrounded by glorious elm trees: tall, stately and symmetrical, their thick, dark green foliage reaches almost to the ground. Through the elms at the farther end, one glimpses some low, rambling buildings, their walls dazzlingly white, and their roofs of red tiles. With the sun shining and bringing out the colours, the whole picture was one to worship.

I love every step of the walk from the second lock to the old Dock House – I like to see the still, placid greenness of the canal, not too green to mirror the house or the vivid flowers which grow around it, and the lovely willow trees. It always cheers me to walk along that canal bank.

Well, Diary, it is nearly five o'clock, I shall have to be laying the table for tea in a moment. Peggy and John have gone to play down at the dock; they are very excited because Daddy has made them a new raft to float on. I should adore to float along the canal, I must go down there soon. I expect they will be surprised – they think I am so superior! Little Thurston James and Philip Metcalf have now followed them down there to share the fun. I hope they will not drown themselves, but Daddy is there, so there is no danger.

TUESDAY 20 AUGUST 1918

THE SKY WAS grey and gloomy, and until about ten o'clock it rained almost all the time. While the weather was in this state, I did my household work, mostly sewing, which is worse than anything else, I think.

About half past ten it was not raining, so Peggy, John and I went down to the dock, wearing our mackintoshes. We found a little boy called Tom Stone, a little girl and Frank Airey already on the raft. So, we three got on, and took it in turns to punt along the canal, quite close to the bank. I enjoyed it ever so much.

I simply love water; somehow the raft and the canal are the realisation of my childish dreams. When I was little, I always used to long for a stream or a brook, or a pond – any water, in fact, that would be deep enough and sufficiently large to allow me to float a boat or raft on. I never got it: and I dare say that even if a stream and a little boat had magically appeared in our back garden, I should never have been allowed to go near it. Now, the opportunity has come, and I am almost too old to appreciate it – not quite, though, thank goodness!

WEDNESDAY 21 AUGUST 1918

PEGGY WENT DOWN to the dock about quarter to twelve, to give Daddy his lunch. Soon after, I began the preparations for dinner. I got the potatoes cooking all right, but alas! I failed over the kidney beans! I put them, all nicely sliced, in a large saucepan and filled it with cold water. Then I staggered to the gas stove with it and lit the gas under it. I knew I had to put some soda with them, but how much? 'A piece the size of a nut', I had heard. Yes, but what kind of nut? There are nuts and nuts, coconuts and hazel nuts! My inclination was towards the latter, so I put in a piece about the size of one.

This, I found subsequently, was right, roughly speaking. But alas, when Mother came home, she almost fainted on hearing that I had put the beans in cold water. They should only be put in when it is boiling. Fortunately, they were not quite spoilt.

During dinner I wondered what I could do to help me to recover somewhat from my trying experiences as house-keeper. I decided to go for a walk in the fields by myself, taking only a book for company, so that I could sit down in the shade somewhere, and not feel lonely. So about quarter past two I dressed in a cool old white dress, and started off.

I went up the high fields and walked through them until I reached the road that runs along the other side. It was a glorious afternoon; the sun was shining in the cloudlessly blue sky, while a delightfully cool breeze was blowing. The 'high fields', as their name shows, are above the level of Llandaff and Whitchurch. The breeze blew freshly upon them, while from where I stood, I had a lovely view of the hills around Taff's Well. The fields in front of me, with their soft carpets of green grass, and high, shady hedges, looked inviting, but – 'Trespassers will be prosecuted'! There was no irate farmer, nor any farm hands about, however, so I scrambled over a rough fence, and crossed the field.

Why is it that there is so much pleasure in doing what one ought not to? I strolled along in the shade, enjoying the sensation to the fullest. I had just discovered that the green colour was the result of cabbages, when coming to a gap in the hedge I found two men – the cabbage keepers, presumably – regarding me with intense interest. The only thing to do was to walk on steadily, unconcernedly, with the carefree aspect of the innocent. So I did, stifling at the same time an unworthy temptation to turn and run – anywhere, out of their sight.

About four o'clock I settled myself with 'Henry Esmond' under the shade which the cows enjoyed. I leant against the trunk of the tree and made myself comfortable. The cows came to look at me, with interest. One gave me an uncomfortable five minutes, by approaching very near and gazing at me with a look that seemed distinctly hostile. I returned his stare, pondering the while on the best way to run should he cease staring and endeavor to come to business. My meditation was needless – my stare seemed to discomfit him, he turned his back upon me, to my relief.

THURSDAY 22 AUGUST 1918

DURING BREKKER, MOTHER said that Peggy, John and I had to go to pick blackberries. While Peg and I did some housework, Philip Metcalf and John started on the quest. They came back with – none. Peggy and I went, and roamed for a few hundred miles, I should think. I enjoyed rambling in the country, looking for the berries. It was a lovely morning, the sun shining in a cloudless sky, and everything was fresh and green. With much labour and difficulty, we managed to pick half a basketful of blackberries, and returned home, very hot and tired, about one o'clock. On the way back we met 'Ginger' or Donald Wallace (what he is like you can guess from his nickname), and 'Pecker' or Cyril Morgan, the affection between whom and my sister is well known.

After dinner we decided to laze. But I had first to write to Hilda Davies, so went to the breakfast room to do so in peace and quiet. Alas, Philip Metcalf came in. Exit peace and quiet! He tried to get you, Diary dear, and I had to fight him to get you back. He took my pencil and rubber, he read Winnie Platt's letter, and when I locked him in the conservatory, he began taking off my bicycle wheel. It was four o'clock before he left. You can imagine my tremendous relief!

SUNDAY 25 AUGUST 1918

I AWOKE THIS morning with the sense of discomfort which a cold always brings, while the weather was not of a cheering nature. I knew there would be no chapel for Peggy, John and I, so lay dreaming until about half past nine. Then, when I got up, the rain was descending, now in a blinding mass, now in a gentle drizzle, from a somber dark sky. Everything seemed gloomy. We had a ripping dinner about one o'clock, it was so excellent that it cheered us all somewhat.

After tea Daddy went to chapel, and I went to play hymns in the drawing room. I do not think that there is anything in the world so stirring and so strangely moving as the old Welsh hymn tunes. Whenever I hear the solemn cadences of such old hymns as 'Aberystwyth' and 'Cwm Rhondda', something in me seems to quicken in sympathy.

The Welsh are always moved by the old hymns. I remember a week or so ago, Daddy was speaking of the Cymanfa

Ganu which followed the Eisteddfod. There a huge number of Welsh folk, many thousands, sang the most famous of the old tunes, all in Welsh, the echoing and reverberating Welsh, and with such fervent enthusiasm, the sound must have been beyond words. As Daddy spoke of it, he was transformed, he was almost shouting as he described it, and with his hands beating time to 'Cwm Rhondda', his blue eyes were flashing fire. It seemed to me so typically Celtic and made me excited to watch. We catch fire so easily.

MONDAY 26 AUGUST 1918

I AWOKE THIS morning to find the clouds had broken and the good old Sun was beginning to assert his sway. I recollected as I dressed that it was 'Black Monday': I had to collect the rents. This cast something of a damp over my cheerful spirits.

After brekker, I helped Mother in the house. Then about eleven o'clock I had to start on my toil. I usually walk to the Freehold full of the blackest care and anxiety, but this morning everything was so fresh and joyous that I could not worry, somehow. Perhaps this helped me – anyhow, I got the money quite right, really Diary dear! It is such a rare happiness for me, poor me, to get the rents absolutely correct.

That troublesome spirit, Mrs Maloney, paid nine shillings today. She is now one pound and two shillings in arrears. I hope that she is reforming. Anyhow, I can't for the life of me say anything to her. How could I, when in the room, on a bed, lies her child, the most pitiful little object you could imagine – white, and very, very wasted, a weak little shadow, with pitiful dark eyes? And Mrs Maloney's husband is dead. What a lot of suffering there is in the world and what a lot of heroic struggling, on the part of weary-eyed, tired mothers to 'make the two ends meet'. But that sort of heroism goes without record.

When I first began to collect the rents, I used to look for little bits of loveliness in Nature, for trees dancing in the sunlight, for a patch of blue sky. The sight of these seemed to refresh and to comfort me. Now I take more interest in the people themselves. I am happy in possessing relatives of very strongly marked personalities. For instance, could you find another man like Uncle Davey? He is a prodigious reader of abstruse theological works, he is a leading light at a Calvinistic Methodist Chapel; yet he behaves in a most unchristian way towards his brother, Daddy: he breaks his promises, never by any chance pays for anything he purchases, and when the creditors come to him, he rants and raves, and so abashes them that they retire as if they were the guilty persons. Yet he once told Daddy that his name was 'Mr Pay-Tidy'!

When Harold Airey died, he refused permission for the funeral to pass through his fields, although there was no other way except by the canal bank. An old friend of his went to ask permission: he raved at her. Finally, he said 'Bury him in the back garden! Or float him across the canal!' This kind of thing belongs to the Middle Ages, the Dark Ages. Yet he has a most winning manner, and way of turning his sentences, which is purely delightful! Then Aunt Polly; she of course is unspeakable.

Now, where have I wandered to? Oh – I remember – well, I collected the rents, then went home. After dinner, I had to go to town. I put on a new costume, rather a pretty one, much too pretty for my face, and caught the half past three train. I went to the bank and got Daddy's bread from the Carlton.[12] Went home by the half past four and had tea about five o'clock. I heard the sad news that Nicky Metcalf had fallen into the canal from the raft but had been rescued. John was wishing it had been him who had fallen in, silly child!

TUESDAY 27 AUGUST 1918

DADDY TOLD ME that I had to go to town, to collect the rent for the garage from the Treforest Electrical Power Company. Mother also had a good deal of work for me to do, so I was busy all the morning. We hope to go away soon, and there is a lot to be done before we leave.

It rained intermittently all the morning, and after we had dinner, it descended in a steady downpour. As it was so wet, Mother said Peggy and John could come with me, and that we could all go to the cinema. So, we caught the half past three train and went to the offices of the Treforest Electric Company. They are at the top of a many-storied building, and as the lift was not working, we had to toil up a few million steps to get there. We clattered down, making

12 The Carlton Café, Restaurant and Hotel, a large and fashionable establishment in Queen Street, Cardiff.

a fearful row on the hard wood, and went to the Park Hall Cinema. The most important picture was a rather novel one, called *The Lust of Ages,* featuring Lilian Walker. 'The Lust of Ages' was of course the lust for gold. The picture represented gold to be at the root of all evils, and showed how the lust for gold in a man could ruin his happiness and ultimately poison his life.

FRIDAY 30 AUGUST 1918

IT WAS A dull kind of morning, rather discouraging when we have decided to go for our holidays tomorrow, isn't it? We must go now, for last night our Sunday school superintendent, Mr Chauveau, cycled down to ask if we were ready to take part in the 'Rally' on Sunday. Full of unholy joy, which showed in a broad grin, I am afraid, I said we were 'very sorry, but we were going away on Saturday, but I hope he would have a nice meeting!' I am so glad to escape singing at Tabernacle! I had an experience of it last year, as you may remember, Diary dear.

By the way, I was reading some of my old 1917 diary a few days ago, and I was struck by my own folly. I think I must have been even sillier than I am now. I hope my 'style' in writing has improved somewhat since that time, too. What do you think, Diary? I wish you could give me your candid opinion.

SATURDAY 31 AUGUST 1918

I AWOKE THIS morning with a delightful feeling of antic-
ipation and excitement, for we had arranged to go away this
afternoon if the weather was good. I jumped out of bed and
ran to the window: above me the sky was a clear deep blue,
but in the north, along the horizon, lay dim ill-defined banks
of grey clouds.

It was a very fresh morning, almost chilly, and Mother
dreads being away from home when it is cold. We had an
experience of it at Bournemouth in the spring. It was very
cold there; every day a bitter east wind was blowing, and
although there were good fires in the drawing and sitting
rooms, our bedrooms were freezingly cold. Mother said hers
was like an icebox, and Peggy's and mine was worse. So I
turned away from the window in a doubtful state of mind.
When I asked Mother if we were really going, she would not
commit herself, but said that if we were, there was a lot of
work to be done.

Then Daddy came in, and after consideration, he and
Mother decided not to go until Monday. I did not mind
particularly, but I was wondering what Mr Chauveau would
think when he saw us in chapel after all.

SUNDAY 1 SEPTEMBER 1918

THE FIRST OF September! Only a fortnight more of holidays! Oh dear, oh dear! I have wasted the month of August:

all the work that I meant to have done I have not touched. I have not even finished *Bleak House,* nor *King John,* and I intended to read so much! Really, Diary, I must believe that I am the most hopelessly lazy person in existence.

I started September by getting up late, as we always do on Sunday. Furthermore, I broke into four pieces a new comb Mother had bought Peggy and me. I caught hold of it and started combing my hair really gently. Suddenly it burst and fell in pieces at my feet. I could not understand it; Mother said she could, when I told her, and was very angry indeed. I thought her anger should have been directed towards the comb and not towards me. So the day broke in squalls.

After brekker, the electricity in the atmosphere was considerably less than before. Peggy and I went to get ready for chapel and wore our new fawn things. We walked around the 'Long Way' since Aunt Polly is away.

Mr Viner was the officiating minister. He preached on the Christian's need for purifying himself every day, for 'washing his feet', so to speak. I enjoyed the lessons; one was a psalm, the one about the Lord being 'refuge and strength' and covering his chosen with his wings. This psalm always seems to me so comforting and reassuring, somehow.

We walked home after the service by the 'Short Way,' and arrived at quarter past twelve. I may say that we had an excellent meal, even for Sunday. After it, we had to go to Sunday School, which was having its 'Rally Sunday', so Daddy came with us. Uncle David was also there, but of course we were not speaking to him. What a hypocrite the man must be! How can he dare to come to chapel, and sit, so assured and comfortable, as if he had never sinned in his life!

Everyone is talking about him and his wild passions. Many people would hate having to bear the same name that he has and being such a close relation, but I don't mind. The friends that are worthwhile will take me at my own value, not that of my relations.

The service was not particularly good. One little boy recited a 'poem' of which every verse commenced 'I am a temperance lad' and then went on in rhymed couplets, such as 'And so too is my dad', 'and of that I am glad.' Another recited Tennyson's 'Crossing the Bar'. How superb that is in its wonderful simplicity, the simplicity of the truly great.

When the 'rally' was over we walked home through the fields; the wind was still blowing, keenly and cuttingly, and the trees were waving and bending before it. After tea, I went to change my dress, and then sat in the drawing room. The Owens were sitting in their front bedroom, and staring down at us, but I was determined not to move because of their rudeness.

MONDAY 2 SEPTEMBER 1918

TODAY WE CROSSED the Bristol Channel and came to spend a week or so in Weston-super-Mare.

We came by the boat which leaves Cardiff at twenty minutes past two, after a busy morning. After brekker I got some clothes ready to pack, then at about eleven o'clock I went to collect the rents. I got home about half past twelve, had dinner, and then Mr Woods came to drive us to the docks. We got on board and had a rough crossing: ever so many people were ill, but I enjoyed the rolling and the strong wind, wet with the salt spray.

When we got to Weston, we had to find rooms, and after much dreary walking on a hot afternoon, we eventually found some at Mrs Madge's. It is very clean and freshly open but is a long way from the seafront.

Peggy's and my bedroom is a tiny little affair, with white distempered walls and ceiling. The bed is small and hard, but not actively uncomfortable. Unfortunately, there is not a single drawer or wardrobe in the room, so we have to hang all our clothes on nails on the walls, over the little prints and texts which are everywhere. Our landlady is a Baptist and has an enormous collection of coloured texts and 'good words'.

TUESDAY 3 SEPTEMBER 1918

THIS MORNING PEGGY, Daddy, John and I had a short walk before brekker. After the meal, the children and I went down to the sands. We indulged in a short donkey ride, which we all enjoyed hugely.

I wish I could say that the sea was clear and blue, dancing and sparkling in the sunlight; but alas, it was far from it, being thick and muddy. Only once have I seen it transformed. This was at sunset, when the sun was still some distance above the horizon, and round about it gathered the clouds, tinted gloriously by its dying splendour. I was delighted to see it so and stepped nearer. Alas, at close quarters I could see it brown and muddy as ever!

WEDNESDAY 4 SEPTEMBER 1918

TODAY WAS WET and gloomy; we decided to have our photographs taken, in a family group. Accordingly, we walked through the town to the Boulevard Studio and posed before the camera. We, that is Peggy, John and I, got the giggles very badly. I could not control myself, despite many little encouragements from my parents, especially Mother; and every now and then I would explode convulsively, then Peggy and John would follow. Nobody's temper was improved by the experience – I am sure mine wasn't. A profound fit of melancholy succeeded that of unseemly mirth, and the weather was also gloomy.

A good dinner cheered me somewhat, and after it I went to Ashcombe Park, a very nice park quite near here. The front part, in which there is an excellent bowling green, is very well kept, and is gay with sweet peas, lobelias, geraniums and snapdragons of every gay hue. These snapdragons remind me of my youth, when I used to play a game with them, which we called 'Snapdragon Hospital'. We used to treat the snapdragons as sick people and put all sorts of concoctions down their throats. John had a long row of very shriveled and withered ones, which he used to endeavour to restore to life and beauty. I may add that he was rarely successful. We older people called his institution 'Sixty-six shrivelled kids!' and pointed derisive though grubby forefingers. Our own establishments contained the select number of a dozen or so:

we went in for quality rather than quantity.

After tea, Daddy and I went to the Pavilion on the Pier to see *The Geisha*.[13] I enjoyed it very much indeed. The music is most delightful and the dresses and scenery pretty and effective.

Some women seated behind us amused me very much with their talk; they were Welsh women, and possessed a very real, though unconscious humour. They talked of their food, the stuff they liked and the stuff they did not like, and the way they liked it cooked, and related many spicy anecdotes of their experiences at other people's tables. One concerned a piece of salmon which the lady did not like, but she was at a friend's house, and had before said how she liked that fish. Fortunately, there was a little dog under the table … I could not help laughing as she related this story in a way infinitely quaint and droll.

I liked Reginald Fairfax, in his naval uniform, and I was absurdly thrilled when he sang 'Star of my Soul'. He had a beautiful voice: rich, deep and manly, and in this song particularly, it vibrates with passion and longing. It made me wonder whether any man will ever care like that for me – be heartbroken when I am in danger or trouble, and valiant in my defence? I suppose these romantic feelings are very silly and girlish; still, I must confess to them.

---

[13] A popular musical comedy first performed in London in 1896.

THURSDAY 5 SEPTEMBER 1918

AFTER BREKKER we went to the Baths, to see how things were arranged there. Mother wanted me to learn to swim, so Peggy and I went in. The water was not very cold, and kicking, splashing, floating and trying to swim, I enjoyed myself ever so much.

FRIDAY 6 SEPTEMBER 1918

THIS MORNING John and I had a splash in the Baths. I had a lovely time going down the chute and trying to swim. I nearly can, now. From the Baths we walked straight home to dinner. After the meal, Peggy, John and I walked to the front. We found a cosy little nook with a seat in it and there I read ever so many pages of *Henry Esmond*. With every page, a sense of virtue and well-doing rose higher within me.

After tea we returned to the front with Father and Mother. There were some people on the sands singing hymns, and try as I would, I could not escape hearing some words of 'Lead, Kindly Light'. You notice that I say I tried to escape hearing; that is the truth, I did. That hymn always disturbs me, and I hate being disturbed. It makes me think of things I would rather forget, especially when I am on holiday.

SATURDAY 7 SEPTEMBER 1918

WE ALL WENT to the Baths in the morning, and I made further progress with my swimming. After came dinner, and then the afternoon spent in Ashcombe Park. Daddy played bowls there with other gentlemen. I sat on a seat, alternately watching him and writing a letter to Jim.

About four o'clock, we walked to the front, and when we were in sight of the sea, Mother recollected that we had Daddy's bread to get. I heroically determined to trudge back to the 'Health Bakery', which lies beyond Holland Street, even. So I went in the rain and was soaked.

SUNDAY 8 SEPTEMBER 1918

AFTER BREKKER, we set forth for chapel. We went to Mrs Madge's place of worship, Wadham Street Baptist Chapel. It is a very nice building, rather dark and gloomy, however. The pastor officiated. He is Mr Turner and spoke very well. His sermon was evidently carefully thought out, and there was no superfluity of language. He emphasised a point which I seem to be always reading in various places, that there can be no general social reform of the community before a regeneration and spiritual rebirth of the individual.

MONDAY 9 SEPTEMBER 1918

DADDY WENT to Llandaff early, to collect the rents, and did not come home until late. Peggy, John and I went to the Baths in the morning. I have been trying to swim every day, and now at last I can get across the width of the water. I am feeling quite proud of myself.

TUESDAY 10 SEPTEMBER 1918

IN THE EVENING we all went to the front and walked together there. The crowds of people continually passing up and down is almost unbelievable. I love to sit on a seat and watch them. You see so many varied types, so many different faces and so many grotesque toilettes, also.

WEDNESDAY 11 SEPTEMBER 1918

WRITING THIS NEARLY a week later, I have forgotten to tell you, Diary, of the good news which came to me on Sunday, the 8th. I had a letter from Vera Shepherd and another from Mabel Roach, both giving me the results of the C.W.B. exams in July. I have passed, with two distinctions, one in French and the other in History.

Of course, I am tremendously pleased, but my first feeling was, most absurdly, one of disappointment! Disappointment when I hardly hoped to get through, even. Yet that was how it was. You see, I wanted above all things to have distinction in Literature and haven't … Oh Diary! And after such a year of work! Yet I can say I have grown, how much you would scarcely believe during the past year; largely owing to the influence of Miss Layton. And this growth is surely the real and lasting end of a year of work. But, still, I would like to have done better in the exams, to crown the work of the year more tangibly, so to speak.

To get back – on Wednesday morning we all, as usual, splashed about in the Baths, and had a very jolly time. In the afternoon, Daddy and Mother went to Clevedon by the light railway. They thought Clevedon was a very pretty little place, but rather quiet. I think I should like it.

THURSDAY 12 SEPTEMBER 1918

TODAY, I HAD my photograph taken at R.W. Brown's studio on the Boulevard, where we had before had our family group. It was a dreadful experience; I was horribly nervous and sure that I would come out like a perfect fright. At last it was over, and I walked with relief to the Baths. There I practiced diving from the deep end and then swimming frantically away. I never enjoyed myself so much.

SATURDAY 14 SEPTEMBER 1918

TODAY WE WENT home by boat. It was a wet, stormy day, and I was not sorry to think we were 'homeward bound'. On Sunday, I suppose I shall go to chapel and Sunday School, then on Monday I shall be very busy collecting the rents and preparing for school, which starts on Tuesday. And I have done nothing to prepare for it. Alas for all the work I was going to do in the holidays, and about which I said so much in the beginning! I have read no Shakespeare at all, and only a small part of *Henry Esmond*. What a record for seven long weeks. Well, it is too late now, the opportunity has been and gone and I have not used it. Alas, once more! Now, on Tuesday, starts the new year of work.

The Tabernacle, Whitchurch

1920

I would rather have a soul, though it must ever be hungry;
I would rather live, though it means suffering ...

The last two diary notebooks

WEDNESDAY 24 MARCH 1920

MY LAST BOOK ended on the 16th, and I have written nothing since, because so little of interest has happened that it seemed a waste of good paper to tell you about these last days. Over the weekend we had glorious weather and on Saturday afternoon we all went for a drive in an Angus-Sanderson car. We have now ordered one and are looking forward to having it in July.

Today it is drizzling rain, all seems dreary and wet. And we had an essay to write in the morning. We were given two hours to write on these lines:

> *'I am the master of my fate; I am the captain of my soul.'*[14]

I finished long before an hour and a half had passed, and only succeeded in writing four pages. Nearly all the others have written eight or nine pages and took the whole of the time. I suppose I shall be bottom. Heavens, I am not looking forward to hearing the results! In my essay I made successful mastery of fate depend upon full captaincy of the soul, or self-control. I quoted those lines of Tennyson, which are very dear to me:

> *'Self-reverence, self-knowledge, self-control – These three alone lead life to sovereign power.'*

Then, directly after finishing, I went to the form room.

---

[14] From *Invictus* by William Ernest Henley (1849—1903).

When the others came down, I joined in the general noisy conversation. Then I remembered how earnest Miss Layton had been last year on this point, of working quietly and steadily after an examination, so as not to disturb others. And I had been writing about the necessity of 'constant and faithful endeavor to exercise self-control in the small, petty affairs of daily life'. I can hear Miss Layton's voice, cold and scornful, and imagine her eyes seeing through me and despising what she saw. For the last free lesson, I sat apart from the others and read Sir Sidney Lee's *Stratford on Avon*. But I must be watchful tomorrow; I must struggle towards self-control.

And today we are having our Inter-Debate.[15] My heart simply turns over when I think of it. For I am supporting a boy in saying that Science has benefited man. I cannot read a paper; I have to speak from notes, and I don't know what to say. I have a horrible feeling that my arguments will not stand and that I will become hopelessly confused and incoherent. Ivy Mundy is writing the paper opposing the motion and Miss Collin seems to have taken a great interest, for Ivy has been given lots of points and has had advice about her paper.[16] This seems to give her rather an advantage. I sincerely hope that I will not make a fool of myself, but it seems almost too much to hope.

(Later) The debate was a great success and most enjoyable. It was very queer to see boys trooping into our nun-like

[15] Debate against the Boys' Intermediate School.
[16] Mary Collin (1860—1955) headmistress of Cardiff High School for Girls and campaigner for women's suffrage. She and Miss Layton had also taught together at Nottingham High School for Girls.

corridors and rooms. Miss Collin came in and was very kind and jolly. She introduced us to the speakers, and then the debate began. Miss Gibbon came in and sat in the back row and then Miss Layton came and sat next to her. Ivy Mundy opened the debate with a very good speech; Mr W.R. Harrison followed her. I liked the look of him, he was tall, dark and fresh-looking, but his voice! It was so deep, and so like a preacher's! Mr Marquand, on the opposing side, spoke very well, in fact so did all the boys.

At last came my turn. I felt strangely calm and collected and at least did not make a fool of myself. Next day, Vera McConochie asked me if I had seen Miss Layton's face while I was speaking. When I said I had not, Vera remarked: 'You ought to have seen it. She looked so pleased. I have never seen a person look so pleased with someone else!' I felt warm and glowing as I heard this. What more could I wish for, Diary? To think that she was pleased!

FRIDAY 26 MARCH 1920

A HORRIBLE French Literature exam: I am sure I have made a hopeless muddle of this, as of the English essay. Oh well!

In the afternoon I went back through pouring rain to Choral. About five o'clock, the weather cleared, and bright sunlight glowed upon the walls and the floor of the hall. Chaucer looked out with his friendly smile, Byron exulted in some long-passed storm, Milton with pensive air mused upon dark and terrible things, while Shakespeare gazed full and serenely upon the play of golden sunshine. The hall seemed suddenly a place of almost sacred rest and peace, like some chapel dim with mystery and remembrance. Miss Layton's spirit seemed very near to me just then. I thought of myself as I was from years ago, a child sitting in the front row at Choral. How much I have changed since then! I love the hall in its afternoon peace, when the sunshine comes creeping in and old memories stir like ghosts.

SATURDAY 27 MARCH 1920

THE WEATHER was wet and stormy, so Vera McConochie and I could not go for a ride together to Saint Fagans as we had arranged. I enjoyed my morning, for I read some excellent notes and extracts from Homer, Pindar and Aeschylus. In the afternoon I rode to Llandaff to see if Vera had by chance turned up. As she had not, I rode home again through the rain.

In the evening, a most distressing thing happened. Peggy seized me and held me on her lap; I just could not get free. Then, when we had fooled around for a time, I noticed that the glass from my watch had gone, and that both its hands were wrenched off. I never felt so wild and so mad with myself as then. To think that I had been foolish enough to destroy my watch deliberately. I was simply enraged. Looking back, I am still ashamed of the exhibition I made.

The rest of the evening was simply wretched: when Mother

came home, and was so sweet, so kind and so unselfish, I felt a perfect fiend, and prayed that I might not be such a fool in future. I remembered, too, that it was just a year ago when I was suffering torments at school, when my order was bad, my self-respect lost, and Miss Layton despised me. When I think of my folly and succeeding passion, I am filled with wretchedness and humiliation. I pray to be helped to exercise rigid self-control in the small things of life, that when I am shaken with passion at a crisis, I may yet keep some measure of dignity, of calm, may yet be 'master of my soul'.

SUNDAY 28 MARCH 1920

TODAY WE HAD the very great privilege of hearing Doctor Gordon Roberts speak. Dr G. Griffiths was the first medical officer sent out to the Welsh Mission at Shillong[17], and he was the first to arrange for medical aid to be given to the Indian people. He built a hospital which was unfortunately destroyed by an earthquake. Doctor Gordon Roberts, a highly qualified surgeon, determined to go out there to carry on the work. He is surprisingly young, a slender man whose fair hair and pale face make him seem even more youthful than he is. He has done magnificent work and has even convinced the Government that a hospital staffed and organized by missionaries, who know the people and their language and have won their respect and love, does far more

[17] The capital of Meghalaya in north India.

and is more useful than a merely state institution.

Doctor Roberts spoke of conditions out there, of the pressing need for medical work, with a very great earnestness and sincerity. He is in England to appeal for funds to build a new Mission Hospital; he has himself given £3000 of his own money towards it and in addition has gained state help and state recognition. He made us all feel that it was our duty and privilege to help him in the great work he is carrying on.

This is the kind of man I could love, Diary. He was not very handsome, but I could love a man like him. I would like to work with such a one, to help and to sympathize with him, to go with him to the ends of the earth if needs be. Are there many such men? I hope I will meet them, for they are the only kind which appeals to me. Mother says that she has always loved doctors, the healers of men, and they seem to fascinate me too.

MONDAY 29 MARCH 1920

EXAMINATION RESULTS WERE announced today. To my very great surprise, I am top in both exams. I have 65 in French Literature and 82 for the English essay. I am not very pleased with the results, but in one way I was agreeably surprised. Vera McConochie insisted that I was lying when I said I thought I had not done well in French: Vera in fact annoyed me very much, as it was really the truth.

We had one free lesson and talked unrestrainedly all through it. I felt weary and disgusted with myself. Shall never forget the agonies of a year ago this time, and it seems to me that I am no better now. Tomorrow is my last chance to vindicate my will: I must keep rigid silence and work hard during the free lessons; I must not talk in the corridors, on the stairs, or in the cloakroom.

TUESDAY 30 MARCH 1920

OUR SECOND LESSON was free. I got out my European History book and began to work. The others talked a lot, but I had determined not to join in, much as I wanted to. Then we had a history lesson and then came Recreation; what a ridiculous name for that stroll round an asphalted playground. But I noticed a dear little chestnut tree in a corner, all green with new leaves. I love the little chestnut leaves, which stretch their tiny parts downwards like five crumpled green fingers. At what are they pointing, I wonder?

This afternoon was glorious; the sun was warm and the air sweet and dry. Peggy and I decided to go for a cycle ride and were joined by Irene Tuckett. We passed down Fairwater Road and followed the road to Saint Fagans. On the way we clambered over a fence into a field, for we saw primroses growing on a bank. Irene is crazy on gathering flowers, and while she and Peggy picked all they could I wandered around. There is a certain fascination in picking flowers, but I always try to resist the temptation. It seems to me greedy and selfish to pick many, and thus rob others of the joy of seeing the flowers, and after all, they look prettier there, on the bank, than anywhere else.

WEDNESDAY 31 MARCH 1920

TODAY WE HAD mark-reading, a fearfully dull proceeding. I was glad to escape from school at about eleven o'clock. Instead of waiting for the twelve o'clock train, I walked straight down to St. Mary Street and took a tram to the top of Cathedral Road. It was such a glorious day that I enjoyed my ride on the front seat on the top of the tram. Then I had a pleasant walk through Llandaff Fields. As I was coming within sight of the cathedral, I passed a beautiful group of trees. Birds were singing joyously; the very spirit of Spring was abroad. Hawthorn is blossoming and the cherry trees are beginning to flower.

Then I found the cathedral open and went in for a minute or two. But there is always such a fusty smell within it that I was glad to escape into the fresh spring air again. I knelt when I was within, but no mysterious sense of reverence crept over me; the proper feeling would not come, and I was obliged to forgo this emotional experience.

In the afternoon Peggy and I rode down to Victoria Park to see if we could get a game of tennis. But the courts will not be open until May. Then, of course, I shall be back at school, and too busy to play. Isn't it melancholy?

THURSDAY 1 APRIL 1920

ALL FOOLS' DAY: the festival which honours us all, as Charles Lamb whimsically remarks.

Such a queer thing happened this morning: I was making the bed, when a shilling fell from the counterpane and rolled across the floor. I picked it up and then – I am going to be frank, Diary, just to show you what depths of meanness there are in me – I debated whether I should keep it and say nothing about it, or whether I should ask to whom it belonged.

I asked everyone in the family; nobody appeared to have lost it, so I said I would keep it. So I found myself in possession of about 1/10d. Some Easter eggs, I thought.

Then, in reading the paper I saw an appeal for help to be given to the starving children of Central Europe. Another severe struggle. Fortunately, I was struck by my pathetic greed, my fatuity in debating whether it should be an unnecessary sweetmeat for an overfed girl or a meal for a starving child … I sent a postal order for 1/6d and have been trying to forget it ever since. I hate the self-satisfied, cheaply virtuous feeling that possesses me after doing what was only my duty. Are other people able to give and then immediately to forget? Or am I unique in my egoism and self-love? I would 'heaps' prefer a frankly selfish person who refused to give, to a person who gave and then glowed for months with a sense of superiority and virtue. My poor Easter eggs have been fruitful in ideas and what queer ones, too!

FRIDAY 2 APRIL 1920

GOOD FRIDAY. In the morning Mother and I went to the cathedral service, which was solemn and beautiful. As on Wednesday, I waited for a sense of spiritual exaltation; it came momentarily now and again, during the anthem and the sermon; then a little of the real Easter spirit crept over me, as the meaning of this festival, joy and sorrow commingled, impressed itself upon me.

SATURDAY 3 APRIL 1920

IN THE MORNING I was busy with housework and errands, and consequently was much gratified to hear Mother – when John had been naughty – remarking that in future we would all have to work on Saturday morning. Hence a slight coolness arose between Mother and myself.

In the afternoon I amused myself by trying to put my hair up. I arranged it in many different ways and looked a freak in every way. It is most distressing, and what I am going to do in the autumn, when it really will have to be bundled up, is more than I can imagine!

How quickly the year has passed, from Easter Eve 1919 to this Easter Eve. And next year …? I often wonder what the future years have in store for me. Sometimes I have a premonition that much sorrow, much failure, much bitterness of spirit are before me. Yet – who can tell? It is a profitless business, this musing on the future, this straining to see what must ever be hidden. I think, on the whole, it is a wise Providence which keeps it hidden.

SUNDAY 4 APRIL 1920

A GLORIOUS MORNING, full of joyousness and the real spirit of reawakening, resurrection. A fitting Easter Morning. We walked to chapel. Alas! Mr Viner was uninspired by the Easter spirit, and delivered, or rather repeated, a series of comfortable platitudes.

I was glad that Communion Sunday happened during Easter week, so that I had an opportunity of commemorating, in the way Jesus himself wished, his sacrifice of himself. I prayed for a closer and more constant communion with Him, that He might be near to me as a friend, as He is to some people. I hate to think that I depend upon Him for the final salvation, for life after death, and yet am so far from Him during my daily life.

MONDAY 5 APRIL 1920

(THE MUSIC SOUNDS a deep note and plays a mournful melody. Enter, with slow and sad step, a girl, soberly dressed, her face anxious and care-worn, carrying a pencil, a book, some money and a little brown bag. She sighs heavily, walks to the front of the stage, and begins to speak …)

Rent day! I started out early, for it was the 'big' day, which means that all the worst people have to be called upon. How I hate them! Especially that fatuous woman who always feigns surprise when I call on a holiday, and who tells me she thought Mr James always made his tenants a present of the rent on such a day. I said that she gave Mr James too little to allow him to do anything of the kind.

'Oh, but look at the lot of money we gives him every week!'

Lot of money! What would you say if you had to live on pre-war rents? How would you like it if your husband had the same salary as before the war? I loathe that woman and others like her. In fact, all people who can only see things from their own particular, narrow point of view! Who would be a landlord's daughter? If ever I write a novel, I shall take a downtrodden and oppressed landlord for my hero, and the bullying, tyrannical tenants shall be the villains, painted in the darkest possible colours.

But to revert to myself (a far more pleasing topic). We attempted a cycle ride in the afternoon, but no sooner had we left Whitchurch than the rain began to pour down. Yet at first it seemed as if the sun were still shining, for hedgerow and field were still tinted with warm colour. And as for the freshness of the air, and the new green! So we rode on, through Llanishen. Then came a terrible shower, we were simply drenched. Through this we scampered home. Still, I had enjoyed the ride. Lilac buds are swelling; fir trees are tinted with fresh green leaves, and the tiny, pointed willow leaves are showing. Everything is joyously changeful. And I live through it all!

TUESDAY 6 APRIL 1920

I CAME ACROSS some of my old diaries and dipped into them for a while. The girl portrayed in the diaries of 1916 and 1917 simply disgusts me. I am filled with bitter shame, mortification and disgust as I read. Why I should feel this unhappy I can hardly explain, but it seems to me that I was very unlovely in character. I suppose I am no better now – still, the diaries of 1918 and 1919 do not revolt me in the same way.

I was particularly struck by the extraordinary way in which I developed between the Summer Holidays 1917 and those of 1918. The change is marvellous, after one short year in the Upper Fifth. I attribute it in all gratitude and affection to Miss Layton. Before that year, I had scarcely come into contact with her; then, she was constantly with us, teaching us History and Literature, and then I began to live.

I can never be sufficiently grateful, nor can I ever estimate how much I owe to Miss Layton. Each time I think of this debt, I am filled with fresh gratitude. And still the ache remains, the sorrow that she is no longer with us. It hurts me when I think of how I have to treasure little meetings, few and far between, when I used to see her several times a day. But it is no good to brood over this; all I can do is to make myself worthy of the friendship I may never gain, by constant work and steadfast endeavour to gain self-control.

ON WEDNESDAY MORNING I went with Mother to town, and had a tooth stopped at Mr Nicholson's, the dentist. One thing compensated me for the pain I endured there and the subsequent weariness of trudging through Cardiff in the rain – I had the pleasure of digging my teeth into a puff stuffed full of glorious Devonshire cream.

Next day, Thursday, I went once more to the dentist's, this time he hurt me more and left me in possession of a sore swollen mouth and a bitter heart. I did a lot of shopping in a rainstorm and arrived home at half past three feeling sorry for myself.

In the evening, I read bits of *Lorna Doone,* which cheered me considerably. Also, I dipped into *Tom Jones,* which had distinctly the opposite effect. I was wondering why it gives me pleasure to read *Lorna Doone* and sorrow to study *Tom Jones.* I came to the conclusion that it is because Blackmore's work is a 'romance'; he does not seek to portray life and human nature as it is. Even the rogues, the Doones of Bagworthy, are not disagreeable; their wickedness has an attractive, romantic flavour which assures us we shall never meet their like outside Blackmore's pages. But in *Tom Jones,* Fielding writes with a purpose – to lash hypocrisy in whatever shape or form he finds it. He portrays life, and as the fact is rarely as pleasing as the fancy, so life is not as attractive as romance. I am awed and impressed when in Fielding's company, but rarely pleased.

Today has been a horrible day. Mother was extremely

depressed as she struggled through the housework, and she talked to me about life in general in such a way as to make me feel utterly dreary and hopeless.

SUNDAY 11 APRIL 1920

MR VINER PREACHED again, which was certainly disappointing.

Uncle Davey has just passed the house; he was walking with a devil-may-care expression, planting his heels down slowly and deliberately. He stared hard at the house as he passed and I, watching, felt a strange yearning towards him, a longing to speak a few friendly words. How sad and wretched it is that a family of brothers and sisters should be thus divided by desperate strife and hatred!

Uncle Davey passed Daddy on the narrow path bordering the canal a few days ago. Daddy said 'Good morning'. His brother did not reply. His sister comes to chapel; after the service she greets the brethren and sisters with enthusiasm; her brother, her nephew and her nieces she does not know. Although in her case I think it is much better that it should be so, for she is not a fit person to associate with. Uncle Davey I think has been largely her tool and I cannot feel the same hatred towards him, rascal though he is. But he is a rascal, nevertheless, and a hypocrite, too.

RENT DAY, as you are probably by this time aware, Diary! Today it was not so dreadful somehow, although I had gone to bed feeling that life was not worth living and had slept so ill that I awoke feeling that it was not worth dreaming away, either. But when I got out, and felt the fresh damp wind on my face, I reflected that it was perhaps better than being imprisoned in the house.

I had a long talk with Mrs Redwood. She is absorbed in the ailments and bodily infirmities – first of herself, second, of her daughter Bessie, third, of her daughter Mrs Cox, whose 'heart is fair broke'.

'I do pity a person as is irritable, Miss James. They can't 'elp it … When a person 'as a complaint in 'er inside, she can't 'elp bein' irritable.'

But I thought her confession that many and many times she has to go upstairs, just to be alone, to be free from the worry of the rest of the family was very human and very touching. I think she suffers much, poor woman.

'A 'appier woman you couldn't wish to find until this complaint took me. Some days I can't do nothink. But there, Lizzie is a girl, a regular outer. Done the bedrooms she 'as – lovely! An' all my curtains she does, a lovely ironer she is, too! But none would ever think what that girl do suffer, through 'er 'ealth!'

And so on, and so on. At last, I managed to escape. Once home, I found that I had collected all the money I ought to have and had not lost any. 'For this relief, many thanks!' I breathed. In the afternoon, to town. Did a little shopping, went to the bank, and thence to the dentist. He re-filled the gaps in my front teeth and pulled out two stumps. I left his house with my mouth full of blood and my heart full of sorrow.

TUESDAY 13 APRIL 1920

I HAD RESOLVED to work all the afternoon and evening, but though in the afternoon I did lots, yet in the evening I did nothing, for Daddy asked me to go to Prayer Meeting with him. So off I went.

The meeting was held in the vestry, a stuffy little room, but – oh joy – from where I sat, I could see through the window a patch of blue sky and a branch or two of apple tree, covered with dancing, fresh green leaves. When the prayers grew too dull, I studied this tiny skyscape, watching it darkening as twilight came on.

Mr Philip Evans read part of a hymn until emotion weakened his voice. I tried hard to sympathise, for he has recently lost his wife, and in a measure succeeded, but still a little doubt remained – how far was all this sincere? Somehow it grated upon me.

When he was praying, there came loud snuffles from a seat near him. I was careful not to look, but afterwards Daddy told me that Mr Apjohn was overcome and was wiping away his tears. And the late Mrs Evans was not his wife, nor any relation, nor even an old friend. Then why such emotion? Such things irritated me, and I was not in prayerful mood. How could I be, when a little in front of me sat Aunt Polly. Aunt Polly at a prayer meeting! 'Save us, Lord, from hypocrisy conscious or unconscious' was the only real prayer that rose from my heart towards that blue and ever darkening sky.

WEDNESDAY 14 APRIL 1920

O DIARY! Have you seen a bunch of dandelions, their flowers like small glowing suns of golden yellow, and their slim, straight stems of palest green? I picked a big bunch of them this morning and arranged them with long sword-like daffodil leaves in a glass bowl. They looked simply splendid on the green tablecloth. Mother came in, saw them, and remarked – 'Oh …! I don't like those flowers,' and she reminded me of the ridiculous old tale which children believe, about the disaster which overtakes people who pick dandelions.[18] I soon realised that she had always despised these flowers; she had never been taught to regard them as beautiful. And besides, they are so common!

This exactly embodies the kind of thing which is constantly annoying me. People, most average persons, accept a certain conventional standard of beauty, for instance, green fields, primrose banks, trees (in the country only), a river,

[18] An old superstition that whoever brings dandelions into the house will wet the bed – which is not entirely far from the truth as traditionally, dandelion was used as a diuretic.

a mountain are to be admired; it is 'the thing' to admire them. But it is rarely sincere, this love of beauty, because most people 'admire' only what is universally admitted to be beautiful. Poets have praised woods and trees, growing in the country, far away from the towns; therefore, people praise such trees. But they never notice the trees which border the streets in the cities. If they truly loved beauty, they could find it and worship it everywhere.

In the afternoon Peggy, John and I went for a ride with Vera McConochie. John was riding a fine new bike. We started from Llandaff and rode through Saint Fagans to Peterstone. I enjoyed the ride very much, though not as much as I would have done had I been alone. Vera looked prettier than usual, but I found her very boring and uninteresting, and I think I must avoid a ride tête-a-tête, which would be even more fearsome. I suppose you think I am unkind and uncharitable, Diary? 'Not more so than other people, but certainly more frank in expressing your opinions.' Thanks, Diary. But you enjoy it, don't you?

FRIDAY 16 APRIL 1920

YET ANOTHER HORRID day! We heard that the committee discussing the Rents Restriction Act had recommended that landlords should not be allowed any profits. I feel too tired to discuss the injustice, the cruelty of this, Diary. It is nothing less than heart-breaking to hear Mother talk: how she and Daddy have slaved and toiled for years and years, have given up youth, enjoyment, everything, for the good years to come. And those years have not come. Instead have come years of famine, to be faced at a time when three children require education.

It is hard, Diary. It makes me feel so hopeless, so discouraged; I do not want to go to college under such difficulties. Mother must have help in the house; servants are expensive. I wish I were the domestic, home-loving type of girl; I wish I could be satisfied to stay at home with Mother, to work with her in the morning, help her to cook dinner; then in the afternoon perhaps go for a short walk with her, then – and so on. But such a life would kill me, Diary, honestly, truly! Even after these few weeks of holiday, I am longing for school. Such a life is so painfully narrow. At first, I feel as if my very soul were bursting; then this passes and a profound weariness, a soul-deadening depression settles upon me, all the vitality seems sapped from me. It is a nightmare. It is more than I can endure.

In one burst of misery, I told Mother that if ever I had a daughter, I would pray that she might not be clever; might be quiet, ordinary, home-loving, contented to stay at home and busy herself about the house. For a woman to be born with artistic or literary talent and all the restless craving that it means, is a curse, a curse to herself and to others. When I said this, with bitter tears in my eyes and a lump in my throat, I meant it, but now – never, never, never! I would rather be as I am; I should hate to live a quiet, cabbage life in 'very great content'. I would rather have a soul, though it must ever be hungry; I would rather live, though it means suffering.

But I wish I could earn some money. We seem to want it so badly. Shall I ever 'make good'? Oh Diary, Diary, how unhappy it all is. Sometimes I feel so tired of it all that I wish for nothing but oblivion, perfect quiet, perfect forgetfulness.

MONDAY 19 APRIL 1920

IN THE MORNING I correctly collected the rents; in the afternoon I went with Peggy to town, to fetch my admission note. Was not very much thrilled at the thought that this was the last time I should do so.

After going to the dentist's, we went to the Park Hall Cinema, and saw an original film called *A Flight to Mars*. Seeing it, I realised how limited is the scope afforded to the writer of film plays, how difficult it is for an idealist adequately to represent his ideals upon the screen. On the film we saw white-robed Martians flocking in orderly crowds, and dancing, but we knew nothing of the work they did; we were left in ignorance as to the rest of the planet, as to whether Mars was inhabited by one people, speaking one tongue, or by different nations. 'What Mars is, the Earth can be' was the moral of the film, and obviously it was intended to herald the new world of peace and goodwill among men. But the canvas is too limited. The cinematograph is a wonderful instrument, but I doubt whether it will ever be a suitable medium for such work.

SCHOOL STARTED TODAY, very calmly and unex-citedly. Miss Gibson gave me a dozen of the Old Girls' Commemoration Magazines and wished me to sell them to girls of the Sixth Form. There was an immediate rush for them; I had orders from every girl, so that I had only two left. I turned to Vera McConochie and asked if she wanted one. To my surprise she said: 'I'll consider it!'

Hastily, I changed the subject. Then we had a free lesson: everyone read their magazines. Vera leant towards me and said quietly, 'I think I'll have one, Mary.' So I handed her one and she read it with great interest, now and again discussing the articles with Eileen Hutchins. At the end of the free hour, she spoke to me again. 'Oh, Mary! If you don't mind, I don't think I'll have one now. You see, I haven't done anything to it.' A pause. 'You see, I'm really stony'.

I told Mother about this; she was extremely annoyed because I had taken the magazine Vera returned to me. She said it was purely meanness that prevented Vera from buying the book and that she had pretended to buy it later, in order to be seen reading one. Then, after reading it, to give it back, when all the other girls had had to pay two shillings for theirs. Mother said I ought to tell the other girls about it in Vera's presence – they have no great opinion of her already and I can imagine what they would think. Still, I should never be able to tell them about it, especially when she was present. How embarrassed she would be! I have not the moral courage to do so!

But earlier in the morning, she had provoked me to plain speaking by sneering at Cardiff University College and remarking how her Scottish friends pitied an unfortunate boy who was compelled to go there. I told her that Cardiff College was a very good one, particularly efficient on the medical side and that it was in bad taste to ridicule it. I added that Welsh people expect people living in Cardiff to show consideration for their feelings. This is only one of many similar instances in which she has been pleased to laugh at Welsh people, Welsh institutions and the Welsh language. I will not endure this kind of thing in a friend of mine and have decided to end all really friendly relations between Vera McConochie and myself.

SATURDAY 1 MAY 1920

THE McCONOCHIE BUSINESS is certainly distressing, but I have stood firm and have made her see clearly that I do not want her friendship. She has not asked for any explanation of my change of attitude; if she does, I shall give her one and that of course will effectually put an end to any friendship between us. Is there any friendship in the world that could stand the trial of frank speech on the part of the friends? I do not believe there is. Restraint and self-control are as necessary in this as in all other things.

I feel very much alone in my form. Vera Newton and Irene are inseparable, Gwladys Evans tends to join them; Eileen Hutchins and Vera McConochie are together, and

Joy Mundy and Edith Stokes seem to be beginning a close friendship. Why am I forever destined to be lonely, to stand outside things? I remember when I was small, I suffered from the same longing for companionship. Actually, I invented a girl, Venetia Greene. I used to write to her, for she lived in – Bournemouth, I believe. Especially in the springtime, I longed for a friend. Shall I ever have one?

Last night I went with Vera Newton, Joy Mundy, Irene Fothergill and Doris Russell to see Martin Harvey in Hamlet. We had good seats in the gallery. I was not disappointed with the presentation: it was excellent. Martin Harvey as Hamlet caught the spirit of the Danish prince, that eager, sensitive, thoughtful and piteous heart. In the first Act, after he had heard the revelation of the ghost, he was particularly fine. His voice and bearing expressed the overwrought nerves, the almost hysterical state of Hamlet. I realised more clearly than before how utterly alone Hamlet is. Everyone seems to fail him, even Ophelia. His mother has failed him; his father is lost to him. Little wonder that he speculates on 'to be, or not to be.'

Ophelia was taken by Miss N. de Silva[19], a lady with a peculiarly cracked and unmelodious voice. She was very good in the scenes where Ophelia's mind wanders; there she seemed to tear at my heart. She reminded me so terribly of Mother, Mother when she lost her reason. There was the same love, infinite gentleness; and the sweet understanding

[19] Also performed as Nell de Silva, born in Chile as Angelita Helena Maria de Silva Ferro (c. 1865—1949), leading lady with her actor husband in their touring theatre company.

gone. I had to come away before the end. I was shaken with terror and pity.

WEDNESDAY 12 MAY 1920

A WEEK TODAY we had Prizegiving, at the Assembly Room in the City Hall. It was quite a grand affair, but to me, most uninspiring. The speeches were all poor, chatty affairs about nothing in particular. Sylvie Chapple, as Head Girl, presented the school's picture to the school, and made a clear, good little speech. I saw Miss Layton at a distance, when a violin was wailing. I was delighted to receive the poems of James Elroy Flecker and the Oxford Book of Verse. Both are goldmines of pleasure.

Next day, Thursday, was wet, Recreation was therefore in the Hall. I was passing in when I met Miss Layton; she stopped and spoke with such sweet cordiality that I felt myself growing warm with pleasure. She asked me to come with a few girls from Whitchurch to the Garth woods on Saturday, to gather bluebells. I was to hear from her about trains and times … Well, I glowed with joy and happiness all the rest of the morning and arranged with the other girls.

But I heard nothing from Miss Layton until Saturday evening, when I received a letter which had been delayed in the post. This was dated Friday and said that she would go to Taff's Well about half past one. I was paralysed with horror – to think of her going there, waiting for us, in vain. I left my tea and flew to Rhiwbina on the bicycle. On the way

I nearly ran into a motorbike – but the accident left me cold. I grinned at the man and hurried on, reaching the garden village in record time. Miss Layton's sister, Miss Herbert, was working in the garden, and she gave me the joyful tidings that Miss Layton had not gone to Taff's Well, owing to the rain. Oh, the relief, Diary!

Miss Herbert took me around the garden, much improved since I last saw it in the autumn, and I talked with her for a good time. She told me that Miss Layton would be coming from Cardiff on the quarter to seven train, so I rode up and down the lanes and walked in the fields until it was time to meet the train. Then I saw Miss Layton and explained to her. She was so dear, and so kind. She took me into her pretty drawing room, then round the garden, and made fun of her newly planted grass plot. It was a great joy once more to hear her delightful little whimsicalities, her quaint remarks. Then she showed me the best way home and talked about another expedition. I was to bring some girls from school to Taff's Well, and we were to meet her there on Tuesday.

Yesterday, Tuesday, Mabel Roach, Elaine Bregeon, Eileen Hutchins and I went to Taff's Well, but Miss Layton did not come. I hope there has been no misunderstanding, and that she is not ill. We rambled in the Little Garth Woods, which are glorious now. Beech leaves and bluebells; saxifrage, ragged robin, violets, a few primroses, strawberry flowers, everywhere. We had two heavy showers, but oh, the freshness of the air, and the sweet scent of bluebells and young bracken after the rain!

We were discussing 'Friendship' in a free lesson today. (I know, I know, Diary. I am backbone-less.) Vera McConochie said she did not want a girl friend, but she had a perfect friend in a boy. Ivy Mundy said her perfect friend was her mother. I said I had not got one, but I thought of you, Diary. I never expect now to find anyone to whom I could tell all the fears that trouble me, all the dreams that haunt me, all the ambitions that possess me. Never, never! I know better now. There is no such thing as a perfect community of souls.

THURSDAY 3 JUNE 1920

TODAY A MOST extraordinary thing happened. It appears that Aunt Polly has started a new campaign against us; her policy has been that of reciting the wickedness and cruelty of Daddy to certain brethren and their wives, in particular Mr and Mrs Apjohn; Mr John Williams and his lady; Mr Henry Morgan and his.

The cruelest blow of all was to her the fact that Daddy ran after a furniture van which was carrying her goods from the Dock House and stole from it a basket of china. The cups and saucers it contained belonged to a set of tea-things given to her by her mother on her twenty-first birthday. This happened in August 1917 and ever since has been so vexing her spirit that she has not been able to commune with her brother in chapel.

She first declared to the pastor, Mr Viner, her intention not to commune until the thief had restored the china. Next, she published abroad all the details of this and other crimes. So eloquent has she been of late that she persuaded three brethren, Mr John Williams, Mr Apjohn, and Mr Morgan, to act as a deputation to Daddy in order to tell him that she was ready to forgive him all the sins he had committed against her provided the stolen china was restored. Daddy had warning that he was about to be approached by these active peacemakers and therefore we were not surprised when about eight o'clock, the three gentlemen came to the side door.

Peggy, a little frightened, took them into the breakfast room. I came in, and was greeted by the brethren, obviously a little ill-at-ease. One gentleman was astonished to see 'what a woman' I was 'growing into'; another started to read John's lesson book. 'What's this? What's this?' he exclaimed. Peggy told him. 'And has John to do that? Poor John! I pity him – poor John – having to learn the nonsense!'

I led them into the drawing room, closed a window and asked them to sit down. Mr John Williams effusively enquired about Mother's health; I replied as briefly and coldly as possible, then went and told Daddy that the deputation awaited him. He laughed for a minute, then washed his hands and walked to the drawing room, shutting the doors carefully behind him. Mother, Peggy and I were left giggling in the kitchen, wondering who would introduce the subject and exactly how he would announce his very interesting text. It was about half past nine when the deputation was finally shown out, taking their olive-branches with them.

Daddy was talking over the meeting afterwards with Mother, Peggy and me. He very rightly despises the tactics of the deputation, inasmuch as they took it absolutely for granted that Daddy was a scoundrel and a thief, who had misused a helpless sister. They made it obvious that they had heard one side of the cause – Aunt Polly's – and that they did not believe in the existence of another point of view.

This attitude, however much it might please Aunt Polly, was not likely to mollify Daddy. He made it clear that he did not accept the absolution so gracefully offered for sins never committed, that he had a strong objection to being called a thief and that friendly relations could never exist between his sister and himself until she had formally apologised for insulting and willfully slandering him. He explained that though he had not thought it proper to inform all the members of the chapel of his domestic affairs, his view of the matter was so different from his sister's that he thought it was his place to offer forgiveness and hers to repent. He did not condescend to explain to them how his sister had done everything, said everything, to make unhappy himself, his wife and his children. Daddy seems resolved not to explain the many humiliations and much suffering which his sister has caused him; I am surprised that he shows such fixed and stern pride. Meanwhile the world, as represented by our chapel, gives its judgment against him.

Speaking to us afterwards, he said: 'I try to bear her no grudge, but she has hurt me. My old friends are not the same. I am the same to them – I act as if I thought they knew nothing, but they are not the same to me. And I know exactly whose doing it is. My place in Tabernacle is very uncertain.' He spoke quietly and laughed as he ended, but I know that he is deeply hurt.

As I sat in the darkened room alone, and the full reali- sation of the horror of her impiety came to me, I cursed the black-hearted fiend from the bottom of my heart. In the dim light I could just distinguish the faces of my grandmother and grandfather in their portrait. One of the arguments brought forth by the deputation was that it was good for Daddy to accept the gracious forgiveness offered by his sister on the grounds that only thus could he hope to meet his father and mother in Heaven! Still, he dared to refuse the pardon, and the deputation turned homewards, consoled for their failure by the thought of the sensational scandal they would be able to weave about the incident for the edification of other charitably minded brethren and sisters in Christ.

SATURDAY 17 JULY 1920

EXAMS ARE ALMOST over, and my school life is drawing to an end. Yesterday I had my last Choral class. I can scarcely realise that I shall never again sit in the hall and sing. Oh the thousands of times I have done it! As I walked home, I tried to picture myself as I was years ago, walking home on a winter evening, a heavy bag of books hanging from my shoulders, a library book under my arm. I used to look forward to Friday evening, for then I could sit and read one of those everlasting school stories.

As I walked home yesterday, for the last time, I felt somehow that there was much suffering and pain awaiting me in the life which is beginning. I felt keenly all my imperfections, my egoism and selfishness and I realised that only pain of the intensest kind can purify me. So be it! If God thinks me worth troubling about, I dare say I can bear it. But I cannot promise that purification, and not bitterness of spirit, will be the result (That shows how far I have to go.) But who knows what lies before me? A few weeks ago, I felt that I was changing for the better, growing a little less bitter, and selfish. Now I seem to have lost all earnestness of spirit, and an ugly, cynical spirit is growing upon me.

Now I can spare no more time to talk to you, Diary, for I have heaps of revision to do.

TUESDAY 20 JULY 1920

THE LAST HISTORY exam is over. I went to it feeling I knew very little and realising that I had no one but myself to thank for that position. I am so extraordinarily, fatally dilatory. Will you believe me when I tell you that I did no work, absolutely none at all, during Friday or Saturday? I began in earnest on Sunday afternoon. Then, when I do begin, I proceed so very thoroughly that I accomplish about a chapter per hour. And when you have to revise a period extending from 1688 to 1900, such a method leaves you little chance unless you begin a month before. Then, at the end of the month, you will have forgotten all you did during the first three weeks.

What am I to do? I grow interested in the revision; I browse over it contentedly, referring to all the history books in the house, going from one to another as a bee flits from flower to flower. Then, about eight o'clock in the evening, a panicky feeling sweeps over me. I work desperately for a while. Then I realise that I must do about three hundred years' history before going to bed, so I sit up until twelve o'clock.

In the night the water tank bursts. (Really, Diary. Wasn't it dreadful?) I crawl out of bed and put my hand to the gap. At last, it is plugged. Then morning light appears, and at half past five I settle down to study the foreign policy of Salisbury, whom the examiner was kind enough not to mention. I did badly at the exam, and all that remains now is a bitter remorse which is like ashes in the mouth. I feel that I have betrayed Miss Layton, betrayed the care and the wonderful teaching she gave us. What a wretch I am!

FRIDAY 23 JULY 1920

ON THIS NEVER-TO-BE-FORGOTTEN day I put up my hair and left school. Yesterday morning we had four free lessons, and we talked all through them. (I don't care, Diary! It was our last chance; we shall all be parting soon.) For the last time we sat in the form-room and discussed things, love and marriage among them.

Enid Stokes and Gwladys Evans said that they are never going to marry; Vera McConochie said she would if she could; I said I would if I could find the great love, the most wonderful thing in the world. But is it in the world? I cannot tell. Anyhow, there we sat and talked, all of us a little sad at the thought of parting, yet all laughing and talking lightly.

But that dreadful spectre of 'things can never be the same again' was lurking in the background.

I think I would like here to put a list of the girls who were in VIA with me.

These were the Arts girls:

Irene Fothergill
Ivy Mundy
Vera McConochie
Eileen Hutchins
Enid Stokes
Gwladys Evans

And these were the Science girls:

Sylvie Chapple
Doris Baker
Vera Newton
Doris Russell

All such good chums, Diary. I loved them all, and only now am I beginning to realise how jolly they were. I shall often long for those free lessons and the unburdening of our hearts. What ripping times we have had, in spite of all the troubles, exams and homework and the rest. I am glad to think that we have arranged to meet on 2 January 1925, at three o'clock near the Castle. I wonder how many will be there? All will be, I hope.

We arranged to put our hair up for today; all the Arts girls did so, but only one of the Science division kept her promise. It felt so strange to have to pass all the girls with a bun wobbling on the back of your head, and your neck feeling strangely exposed. I have resolved not to put mine down again; then, by the time September comes, I shall have grown quite used to the sensation. It feels more comfortable already. I dress my hair in a coiled 'bun' at the back of my head; I hope I look dignified and stately.

So, my school days end on this dull, wet July day. This is the end of Chapter Three, Book I. Now we turn over the page, you and I together, dear. What shall we write upon it?

Diary Entry, 3 June 1920

James Dock House c.1880. Lock house in the
background, Lock 47 (provenance unknown)

A NEW PAGE

Chaucer looked out with his friendly smile, Byron exulted in some long-passed storm, Milton with pensive air mused upon dark and terrible things, while Shakespeare gazed full and serenely upon the play of golden sunshine …

Gwalchmai in old age

TUESDAY 27 JULY 1920

HOLIDAYS and housework begun.

FRIDAY 30 JULY 1920

A WET DAY for Mona McConochie's marriage.[20] She must have been very disappointed.

MONDAY 9 AUGUST 1920

I HAVE BEEN thoroughly wretched and miserable during these last days. To begin with, the weather has been very bad. But far worse than this has been the trouble in our home. I don't know whether I have told you, Diary, that Daddy has chronic indigestion, or catarrh of the stomach. He can eat nothing but milk food and broth, and suffers very much.

His temperament seemed to have completely changed; he never sang, or whistled, or even smiled; very rarely spoke. He sat silent and morose, depressed and ill-tempered. I could not understand it; none of us could well explain his attitude, and it made us all unhappy. I was first concerned, then irritated. He would not speak a word to me. I said to him: 'How did you enjoy the Eisteddfod last night?' 'Very

[20] Vera's older sister.

well', he announced curtly. Now usually, such an opening would have led him into a discussion which would last half an hour or more; sometimes he used to sit talking to me in the most animated way possible, his eyes blue and sparkling with excitement. After the Gymanfa (which he went to Barry to hear) I said:

'What was on yesterday? Oh, of course, it was the hymn-singing festival, wasn't it?'

'Yes', he said. 'And it was very good.'

After that he said no more, and I gave up in despair. He took no interest in any of us, or in our doings. We were talking about spending our holidays at Barry; he sat silent until he suddenly said: 'I'm not coming with you this year. I am going alone for a week to the Wells.' No one spoke for a minute; we were all completely taken aback. Then when I tried to make him explain himself, he would say nothing.

Mother was very cross. She works very hard, and is tired and overworked, badly in need of a holiday and rest. She confided in me. She talked about the shortcomings of Daddy's family and of the misery they have always caused her. She made me realise more acutely than ever before their utter wickedness, their careless disregard of common decency, honour and truth, their hypocrisy and their passion for making the innocent suffer.

From them she passed to Daddy; she made me feel that she did not love him at all; she told me of his selfishness, how he used her money and gave her no thanks for it; how he sought his own comfort and pleasure at the expense of hers, how he made life a hard, dreary and unending toil for her. She talked so until my heart was bursting with despair, until I was sick with misery, until I felt that there was no good in men, in earth, nor in heaven. And all the while I was wiping numberless dishes and plates with a cloth that was sodden and wet and the everlasting rain was lashing against the window.

I cannot describe my heaviness of spirit, the helpless misery that encompassed me. My heart ached for Mother, it swelled with pity at the thought of the long dreary years behind. But even worse was the sense that Daddy was unworthy, a mean and selfish man, even perhaps dishonourable. The thought was agony, yet it was not the truth. Tears smart at my eyes now as I recall the agony. I did not know where to turn. All hope, energy, faith and courage were sucked from me as Mother spoke. I felt my little world falling in ruins about me. Mother always has that effect upon me when she confides in me; she seems to sap all my vitality. I felt all love for Daddy going. I tried feebly now and again to defend him, but they were at best half-hearted attempts.

Then, this Monday morning, Daddy had to go to collect the rents. The increase of 30% was due. A sick remorse and pity rose within me as he left, and I thought of all he had to face. A month ago, he served notices of the increase upon all the tenants; he himself worded and wrote out the increase. All the tenants knew that such notice was illegal; that a printed form, specially prepared, must be used. Not one told Daddy. When he asked for the increase this morning, everyone refused to pay, on the grounds that the form of notice was irregular. I feel too sick at heart to comment on this, Diary.

Then, every man who was paying more than the standard

1914 rent declared that he would recover from Daddy every penny that had been paid in excess. Thus: a certain Mr Roberts came to Daddy in 1915. He was willing to give anything for a house; he willingly, gladly, agreed to pay seven shillings per week instead of six shillings and threepence, the usual weekly rent. Now this man comes to Daddy and demands seven guineas. He will be paying no rent until January 1921. Daddy showed him the form demanding the increase:

'Now, if I were to say to you "pay me eight shillings, instead of seven shillings and ninepence" and you agreed, and paid; then suppose we were to fall out, years later; would you come to me and say: "Now, I want every one of those threepences I paid you?"'

'Oh!' exclaimed the man, a young man, the clerkish type. 'That would be a dirty trick. No one would be mean enough to do that!' 'That is just what you are doing now,' Daddy said. This is perfectly true, Diary. Does it not fill you with consuming wonder?

Daddy brought home the orthodox demand forms; they look fearfully technical and difficult. 'I can't fill them up,' Daddy said hopelessly. 'I don't know how to fill them up.' It seemed as if things were going beyond him; he felt beaten and helpless, and I – I felt sad and remorseful. So, I took the forms and the copy of the Rent Act and worked until I had found the meaning hidden beneath the obscure legal phrasing. Daddy and I went over it together and I think I made it clear.

He told me what had happened, but as he spoke, I felt new courage and hope coming to me. My heart swelled with pride as I listened to him. He took it all so pluckily, so manfully, Diary! He talked quite quietly and would listen to no abuse of the tenants. It must have meant a great effort of will and self-control, for he is passionate and easily roused to anger. As he talked, I often had to struggle hard to keep my own self-control; not so much because I was moved by the attitude of the tenants, but because I hated myself and my unworthy doubts of him. He is so courageous, so plucky. He realises the worst, yet never loses heart. As he talks, he makes me feel that whatever comes, I can face it. I am inspired with a little of his courage. It is a fine feeling, Diary.

He said that the business would mean a loss of fifty to seventy pounds. I said I wished I could get that scholarship, which is worth about sixty pounds. He exclaimed hastily:

'Oh that! Never mind about that! That's nothing', and then went on to talk about something else.

His attitude only makes me feel more and more anxious to win it, to help him in some way. He may be a little selfish, but in essential things he has never been anything but the soul of generosity to me. I have had the best education possible; given, not grudgingly, nor out of a sense of duty, but freely, gladly. When I ask for money for books, he never has enquired 'Are you sure you have bought all the secondhand ones possible?' He has never grumbled but given freely. And he is brave; he can look on tempests and not be shaken. He never loses his head; he is cool in an emergency, sure to do the right thing; he is hard-working and there is no littleness, no pettiness in his nature. He is a dear; he is my father and I love him. All I pray is that I may always be loyal to him in word and deed.

WEDNESDAY 11 AUGUST 1920

I HAVE SUCH stacks of work to do, Diary. I really don't know where to begin. You see, there's a Scholarship Exam beginning on the sixth of September; for that I have to swot up French, English, History and Geography. Then, on the 20th, I go up to Aberystwyth, and there sit an exam in French, English and History. And there are essays in both cases. And I have my clothes to get ready. And we are going to Barry for a week or a fortnight. Is it not appalling? I shall be a pallid, nerve-racked ghost by September 25th. Perhaps I shall not even be alive at all.

MONDAY 23 AUGUST 1920

WE HAVE BEEN staying at Mrs Mumford's, 14 The Parade, Barry, for rather more than a week. We have a delightful place to stay, the house overlooks the sea, and the landlady is kind. But the Stevensons are also staying here and during this first week have dogged our steps and have wearied and irritated us by turns.

At first their liveliness pleases, but later one begins to see that they are continually talking either of themselves or other people. Moreover, their conceit and self-satisfaction are only equalled by their venomous jealousy of others. They have not a good word to say about anyone; everybody is in turn dissected and shamefully slandered. They are positively dangerous. Mrs Stevenson is the coarsest-mouthed woman I have ever met. Her mind must be a perfect cesspool. I know these are harsh words, but they are true, Diary. Sometimes I feel I would give all I have for the privilege of telling Meta, Kathleen and their mother exactly what I think of them. But this cannot be, so I have to exhaust my fury upon you, Diary.

MONDAY 30 AUGUST 1920

NOW WE ARE at home, after what was, on the whole, a pleasant holiday; the weather was good; we bathed, played tennis and went for walks. But I must not indulge in memories of our holiday. Today I am starting work in earnest, for a week today the examination begins. Everyone seems eager that I should gain a grant or a scholarship, or something, and I feel that much depends upon it. There is a tremendous amount of work to be done and little time in which to do it, so you will see little of me for the next week.

WEDNESDAY 1 SEPTEMBER 1920

YESTERDAY I REALLY worked hard at Geography, though of course I was not able to accomplish a quarter of what I must get through before the exam. Peggy was unwell during the day and towards eight o'clock I too began to feel queer. My throat was sore, my head and back were aching dully. I went to bed feeling as if I were going to have influenza. I

dreamed excitedly during the night and awoke with a headache and general feeling of heaviness. I could not get up, so
lay in bed and thought of the work I ought to be doing.

John went into Cardiff to see the C.W.B. results. Junior
results are not published until tomorrow, but he said that my
record was –

French, with conversational power.

History, with Distinction.

English Language and Literature, with Distinction: can
hardly believe it!

Anyway, I do not deserve it. I am going in tomorrow to
see how the other girls stand and whether it really is true
or not. I still feel rather queer; it is now five o'clock, and I
have done no work. John yesterday called me a 'courageous
sticker'! Some reputation, isn't it? I only wish I deserved it!
But yesterday I was in the mood for work and really was
swotting hard when Fate intervened. I think it was really
unkind of Fate, don't you?

THURSDAY 9 SEPTEMBER 1920

TODAY THE EXAMINATIONS ended, to my great relief.
I had the worst of luck in revising. I was ill again on Saturday,
and on Sunday too was able to do little. Wasn't it dreadful? I
felt positively despairing.

The French exam paper on Monday afternoon might
have been worse, but I was not feeling very fit. I felt shaky
about my Geography; shakier still about Literature and as

regards History I was in a state of positive collapse. Then, on Monday afternoon, I found waiting for me the most warm and delightful note from Miss Collin, telling me the gladdest news. I have been recommended for Miss Layton's Prize for English and History. I am so pleased, Diary; that prize above all others I should love to have.

The Geography paper I would have liked very much had I known the work thoroughly, but I did not. As it was, I did the best I could. I should think I should get half marks on the paper. Then we had a good choice of subjects for an essay. I wrote on 'Man never is, but always to be blessed', and preached the gospel of 'Living in the present' and 'Finding beauty everywhere' with much zest and enjoyment. The result I think was fairly good, but other people may not think so.

Today we had a lovely Literature paper; no Grammar, and lots of choice. Also, I was able to finish. So I feel fairly happy on that score. But so too does everyone else!

The History (in the afternoon) I did not care so much for. We had to answer seven questions in three hours; that is rather too much. Still, considering I did not know my work, it might have been much worse. Now I can only wonder. For Daddy's and for Mother's sakes I would love to have a scholarship, of course. But I dare not hope.

A week next Monday I shall be going up to Aberystwyth to sit the scholarship exam there, so next week I shall have to start work again. No rest this side of the grave!

FRIDAY 24 SEPTEMBER 1920

SINCE I LAST talked with you, Diary, lots of things have happened. To begin with, the car we ordered in the spring arrived a week ago, to our great surprise. The result was that we were able to drive to Aberystwyth last Monday. When Monday came, I felt pleasurably excited, and in no wise disturbed by the knowledge that I had done very little to prepare for the Scholarship examination. We were practically all day upon the road, passing through Cardiff, Newport, Pontypool, Blaenavon, Llangorse, Crickhowell, Rhayader and countless other places. Frankly, I was tired of motoring by the time we reached Aberystwyth.

Once in Aberystwyth we drove to Carpenter Hall, where I was to stay. It is on the seafront, near the bandstand. As I said goodbye to Mother and Daddy, I did not feel in the least inclined to weep; in fact, as I climbed the stairs towards the bedroom I was sharing with another girl, I felt exhilarated at the thought of the adventure beginning.

In my bedroom I felt afterwards a little desolate and lonely and dreaded the ordeal of entering the common room. But as I was going down the stairs, a lady introduced herself and her daughter to me. So Ellaline Thomas and I went in together and sat and talked. She was a dark-eyed, merry little Welsh girl. I liked her very much.

We had supper in the dining room. About quarter past nine I went to bed, for I was tired and had a headache. My roommate, Gwyneth Jeremy, came in when I was in bed. Her I found to be very fond of English, and in general a kind and pleasant companion. But as she had two friends from school with her, we did not become as friendly as we would have done had we been alone. The girl I became most intimate with was Mary Phillips. She is a Welsh girl taking the same course as I, which drew us together. All the girls I found to be very jolly and friendly.

I came home by train; walked to the station with Ursula Ellis, another girl I liked, and travelled to Carmarthen in the company of Connie Edwards. She was a short girl, who had bobbed her dark hair, and the fashion suited admirably her pointed little face and soft brown eyes. She, too, charmed me. There was something extraordinarily winsome about her.

Now I suppose you are thinking, Diary, 'What a queer creature! She tells me about everything but the actual exams!' That's coming, Diary.

Now, to begin – on Tuesday, from 9:30 to 12:30, we had English. The paper was moderately decent, and though I could not finish, I feel I did fairly well. In the afternoon we were given two hours in which to write an essay. This paper was not as satisfactory. In the first place, I require three hours in which to write an essay; in the second, I require a decent, interesting subject. There was none such on the paper. After much thought I decided to write on 'Forces which influence national development'. Then I had to think it out. This was such a harassing business that it was long before I started to write. Hence, I had not time to finish properly. Of the general effect of the whole, I dare not think.

In the evening, from 6 to 9 pm we had our History paper. To my astonishment, I did not feel in the least tired, but was quite ready and willing to deal with historical problems.

I wrote, not in the laboured fashion of the afternoon, but with real zest and enjoyment! Moreover, I was able to finish. I think I did fairly well, but in a world where I can get 76 for French Conversation when I expected 30, it is best to say little.

Of the French paper I must say even less. The translation into French was idiomatic; that into English awkward; the grammar was vile and the subjects for essay thoroughly dry and uninteresting. I was bored and sleepy and my work worthless.

As for Aberystwyth, it is a beautiful place. The sea will be a source of never-ending pleasure to me. After the Channel, it is unbelievably clear and its colours – blues, greys, and purples – are splashed from faery palettes. But I know I shall be hungry for sweet country scents and sounds. I must seek the open country, or my soul will starve for the sight of green fields and trees, for the smell of the earth and the flowers, for the glory of autumn in the woods. But on the whole, I came back from Aberystwyth feeling glad that I was to return. I am longing to begin work there.

By the way, I have not told you of the first day at school, have I? Well, I went back, and saw all the dear girls and the mistresses. Miss Woodward gave me some work to do; then we went to hear Miss Collin reading marks. I had some surprises! For French Conversation, for which I had expected about 20, I had 76! And I was in such a stew about it at the time. Then for French Literature, in which I thought I had done well, I had only 60! I had only three more marks for the Literature than for that terrible Grammar paper, while I had 69 for translating English into French, and only 57 for the

French into English. These results simply amaze me.

I was first in three out of the four English exams, and in two of the three History papers. Moreover, I was first in the general totals. I was genuinely and honestly surprised. Of course, this sounds more wonderful than it really is, for you must remember that Sylvie had fewer papers than I, and that positions were taken not on the average, but on aggregate marks. The fact that I had gained Miss Layton's prize for the 'Best and Most Original Work in English and History' gave me far more pleasure, for I felt I had – thanks to the giver of the prize – in some measure deserved it, although you know, Diary, better than most, how 'original' I am.

I was glad to end my school days fairly creditably, but I felt awkward in the midst of what seemed strange and borrowed glory. Honestly, Diary, I feel happier and far more comfortable in the background. All this savours strongly of hypocrisy, but I am for once sincere. I met so many girls at Aberystwyth who love Literature, and who know so much about it, that there is little temptation for me to think myself a prodigy. And here I am turning over the last leaf in this book; soon the tale of one more part of the life in which I am so intensely interested will be told and another chapter begun. I want to go filled with a determination to work hard and to play hard; I want never to forget the beautiful prayer Miss Collin used to recite:

'Enable us to labour diligently, not with eye-service, but in singleness of heart; remembering that without Thee we can do nothing, and that in Thy fear is the beginning of wisdom. Open Thou our hearts to know Thy marvellous

works, and to understand the wondrous things of Thy Law. Of Thy great goodness, pour into our hearts the wonderful gift of charity, and grant that in meekness, truth and purity we may glorify Thee, the Father of Light, through Thy blessed Son, the Light that lighteth every man.'

I would wish this passage to be a 'lamp unto my feet' during the years that are to come. I want to have a deeper, more living faith; I want to be purged of this bitter, mocking, egotistical spirit; I want to be charitable towards men; I want to be good! Oh Diary, Diary! What do the years hold? But it is useless to think of the unknown future, and after all, it is not the life but the living that counts. I must keep my soul, for 'what shall a man give in exchange for his soul'? Keep it, moreover, pure and unspotted from the world. For this, I must learn to ask God's help; upon this, I must learn to ask God's blessing.

Now goodbye, my little Diary-friend.

Mary James
September 27th 1920

EPILOGUE

MARY WAS UNDULY modest about her performance in that gruelling final round of exams: she won not just one scholarship but two, covering the whole three years of her university studies. We know little of her years at Aberystwyth – there is no evidence she still kept a diary – except that she served as president of the Christian Union and studied Political Science, gaining her BA degree in June 1923. No doubt she was proud and delighted to be one of the first women to study in the world's first department of international politics, only recently established at the end of the First World War 'to help the world understand the world'.

Before leaving Cardiff High School, Mary made a pact with her Sixth Form friends that they would all meet up at Cardiff Castle at three o'clock on 2 January 1925. But if any of the girls remembered that date and attended the reunion, they did so without her.

On Tuesday 4 September 1923, she drove down to Llantwit Major with her father, Peggy and John, for an early evening swim. The tide was out and the young people went to bathe almost immediately, while her father sat on the rocks, talking to some friends. Less than five minutes later, cries were heard and it was obvious that both Mary and Peggy were in difficulties. Mary, a strong swimmer, had swum out quite far, and Peggy and John, believing it would be safe despite the undercurrent and waves, followed her, only to find that they were out of their depth. Peggy at first held on to John, but Mary returned to help her, turning her on her back and holding her above the waves. John managed to return to shore and call for help.

Mary continued to hold her sister above the water until a huge wave threw her on to some rocks. She was knocked unconscious by a blow on the chest, while the same wave propelled Peggy towards Henry Millichamp, a brave passer-by who had come to their aid and was swimming towards them.[21] As Henry brought Peggy to safety, her father and another man rushed past him into the sea, asking if he had seen Mary. They found her floating in the water and between them brought her ashore, where artificial respiration was applied for more than half an hour. But to no avail: Mary had saved her sister's life but paid with her own.

Given Mary's love of swimming and the water, often expressed in her diary, it seems particularly cruel that this is how she should have met her death, just as her cousin Betty had done in 1918. Her family's heartbreak never abated, and to the end of his life, her brother John, the guardian of these diaries, could not bear to reveal their existence or to share his memories of his sister.

Mary's mother died six years later, and her father in 1944. By that time, he was living alone, still in Station Road, Llandaff and John, an Army medical officer, was a prisoner of

---

[21] Henry Millichamp (1868—1969), a gardener employed at Llantwit Major, had been a sergeant in the Royal Artillery in the Great War and received the Belgian Croix de Guerre. When commended by the coroner for rescuing Peggy, he replied 'Thank you sir, but I only did my duty.'

war, having been captured at Dunkirk. After the war, John practised as a GP in Cardiff for many years. Peggy, a talented artist, married a Liverpool shipping agent, but was widowed at a young age. She remarried a sea captain from New Quay in Cardiganshire, where she died in 1989.

Readers will notice that there are no diary entries for the period between December 1918 and March 1920, despite a couple of references by Mary to diaries written during this period: we do not know what happened to these. Perhaps Mary destroyed them as unwelcome reminders of a turbulent period in her adolescence, before the influence of Miss Layton transformed her into a serious student. That we have the diaries at all seems a small miracle to us, her relatives. They were discovered in a wardrobe in John's house soon after his death in 2004 by his granddaughter Erin James, and came as a complete surprise. Written in school notebooks, initially in pencil and later in fountain pen, in Mary's racy handwriting and with a minimum of corrections, they are the epitome of a family treasure.

Mary's power as a writer takes us, as in the best diaries, right inside her head. She uses her diary as a confidant and, one senses, as powerful therapy to cope with her difficulties. Idealistic and opinionated, she never minces words and has an endearing tendency to moralise – before pulling herself up short, citing her 'namesake Mary Bennet'. There is a great deal of humour in the diary (both deliberate as in the lampooning of her relatives, and inadvertent, as in the Leonard Jotham episode) as well as a cast of eccentric and memorable characters.

Through it all, Mary's voice is unrelentingly her own.

She has shared her dreams, her growth, her loneliness, her fears of life and death, and her moral struggle; and yet always she returns to a powerful sense of optimism with inimitable courage.

What might Mary have achieved had she lived? Might she have continued writing? Or become a teacher or academic? Liberal politician? Leading official of a Missionary Society, or perhaps herself a missionary?

It is as Mary herself wrote on the last page of her diary: *'What do the years hold? It is useless to think of the unknown future, and after all, it is not the life but the living that counts.'*

S.J.

...he primary schools inspectors under the
He Glamorgan Education Committee.

GIRL GRADUATE DROWNED.

Miss Mary James,
B.A., of Station-road,
Llandaff North, who
was drowned in the
sight of her father
whilst bathing at
Llantwit Major on
Monday evening.

Miss Mary James,
B.A.

420,000 A PENNY.

GERMAN MARK'S RECORD SLUMP.

There was a further...

The Western Mail, 6 September 1923

IN MEMORIAM—MARY JAMES.

The close of the summer holidays was saddened by the tragic news of the death by drowning of one whose name was dear to us all, both for her personal qualities and for her brilliant intellectual promise. Mary James left the School from the Upper Sixth Form in 1920, and having gained a School Leaving Exhibition, and an Entrance Scholarship to University College, Aberystwith, and also a State Scholarship, she entered Aberystwith College. She gained the degree of B.A. this summer, and it was her intention to return for a fourth year for further work. The news that she had met her death while bathing at Llantwit Major came as a great shock. During her school life she had gained the affection and admiration alike of her fellow students and of her teachers, who looked forward confidently to a career of distinction and usefulness for her. In the school debates Mary James was a leader, thoughtful and vigorous. She was the first to gain the Marion Layton prize for English. In our Pageant of Peace at the end of the war it was Mary James who spoke as the Red Cross Nurse, and I shall never forget the impressive earnestness of her voice and look. That her last act was a courageous effort to help her sister is consistent with all we know of her brave unselfish character—short as was her life, it leaves a memory to be loved and honoured.

M.C.

Magazine of the City of Cardiff High School for Girls 1923

ACKNOWLEDGEMENTS

MY THANKS are due to the family of my late cousin Andy James – Gill, Hannah, Nia and Erin – for entrusting me with the task of transcribing and editing these diaries; to Newport Reference Library for the report from the Western Mail; to Glamorgan Archives for permission to use the images of Maplewood, Tabernacle, Gabalfa Dock and the City of Cardiff High School magazine; to University of Aberystwyth Archives for Mary's university records and to David Llewellyn, Nicola Lawson, Pamela Brookshaw, Maurice Gran and Wendy Goldring for acting as 'gentle readers'. Finally, I am extremely grateful to Lorna Brookes of Crumps Barn Studio for her inspirational help in the editing and production of this book.

ABOUT THE EDITOR

SIAN JENNINGS is a retired lawyer and freelance writer who has a Master's degree in Family and Local History and has been actively researching her Welsh roots since 1994. She is the granddaughter of Mary's cousin Madge, who is mentioned once in the diary.

If you loved this book, you'll love
these other history titles:

'Ow Bist?
Ceri Vyner

A personal history of the lost landmarks of Little Somerford.
Who ran the village shop, and where was the forge? What is the
history of the oak tree opposite the Somerford Arms? And what
can a farm pond reveal about Constable's painting *The Hay Wain?*

ISBN 9781915067500

Colkirk Tales
Alfred Absolon

A unique window into life in rural Norfolk before the Great War.
Colkirk is a place where folklore is as real as the seasons and the
harvest is gathered by men and horses, and the village is home to
traditional craftsmen who practice a fading way of life

ISBN 9781915067159

Home Front Wickham
David Warwick

Wentworth in 1939 is a family home in the heart of a
Hampshire village. David's beloved home is soon set to
become a shelter for evacuees from the Blitz

ISBN 9781915067463

Crumps Barn Studio
www.crumpsbarnstudio.co.uk